GOLF FROM THE

CONTENTS	CHAPTER	PAGE
INTRODUCTION………………………………..	………...	1
SHORT GAME………………………………….	I.	4
Putting • Chipping • Pitching		
FULL SWING…………………………………...	II.	32
• Fundamentals • Ball flight laws • Setup		
• Takeaway • Backswing • Downswing • Contact		
• Follow through / release • Finish • Drills		
TROUBLE SHOTS ……………………………..	III.	57
• Sand • Rough • Uneven lies • Wind • Trees		
• Hooks • Slices		
COURSE MANAGEMENT…………………….	IV.	64
ETIQUETTE…………………………………….	V.	67
EXERCISES…………………………………….	VI.	69
PRACTICE………………………………………	VII.	72
EQUIPMENT……………………………………	VIII.	77
RULES…………………………………………..	IX.	78
ACKNOWLEDGMENTS……………………….	X.	80

Steve Dresser's

GOLF FROM THE GROUND UP

This book is dedicated to all the people who have told me "you need to write a book!"

© Copyright 2003 Stephen P. Dresser
2nd edition 2004, 3rd printing 2007, 4th printing 2009
Printed in USA

INTRODUCTION

There is no doubt the single biggest problem for all golfers can be summed up in one word; *inconsistency!* I can't begin to tell you how many times I've watched someone string together a succession of good shots only to say, "Why can't I do this all the time?" I hear it from everyone; brand new players and experienced ones. I honestly believe the culprit is the fact that the ball sits still. Think about it. In other sports like baseball, tennis, racquetball, even bowling, we make motions that are similar to those found in the golf swing. The body rotation is much the same and so is the free swinging of the arms. The biggest difference is that we are in motion and our muscles are *relaxed* and therefore able to function in a reactionary manner. In golf, we attempt to make these same motions from a tension filled standstill and expect similar results. Unfortunately, **you can't think your way through an athletic motion**. So what can we do to make our swings feel more natural? Let's start by accessing the hard drive inside our heads and deleting the word "*hit*." You feel better already don't you? By eliminating "hit" you'll become less "ball bound" and be able to focus on swinging the club, not hitting at the golf ball. You've heard it before. "Gee, you sure have a nice practice swing, why don't you use it when the ball is there?" Most players have no intention of using their practice swing on the golf ball. They just go through the motions without paying attention to what the swing actually feels like. If there were a way to sneak a ball in the bottom of the practice swing, we'd all be golf pros! But alas, as soon as we put the club behind the ball, all those nice relaxed, free swinging motions vanish as we zero in on the ball, our grip tightens, our shoulders tense up and the only thought occupying our minds is **HIT!**

Recently a friend of mine, who is a big athletic guy and former football player, was taking a lesson when he exclaimed "This game would be so much easier if you were allowed to knock someone over!" I thought it was a pretty good line that a lot of people could relate to. He's fairly new to the game and hasn't quite deleted "hit" yet. Once he slows it down a little, he'll do fine. As you read this book, you will notice the word "hit" is used sparingly and rarely in the context of contacting the ball.

Now that you've deleted "hit" from your golf vocabulary you should have more room for the word "**patience**." It's probably the single most important word in golf. It took almost 35 years of playing before I truly began to realize this. I hope it doesn't take you quite as long! Most of us want it all, and we want it now, and if things aren't going our way, we become easily frustrated and begin making poor swings and poor decisions. There is no magic dust or miracle cure for golf. It takes determination and persistence to play this game well. Certainly for some it comes easier than for others but I truly believe everyone has the ability to play golf well enough to enjoy it.

Throughout the years, I estimate to have given lessons to over 20,000 people. I'm often asked if I ever get tired of saying the same thing over and over again. The truth is the golf swing is so individualistic; I don't have to say the same things over and over. If I did, that would mean I'm not paying attention to the uniqueness of each player and I wouldn't be a very effective teacher. Many people have told me they've taken lessons and their game deteriorated or worse yet; they were told they had no chance and ought to consider doing something else. I can't believe an instructor would say that, but it happens. To me, that's a case of an awful teacher, not a poor student. Experience has taught me that when it comes to teaching golf, it's usually easier to talk to the brain rather than to the body, meaning most learn best through visualization. Whether it's a video analysis or one of my crazy props, when I can implant an image in someone's mind, and then allow that player's body to respond to that image naturally, progress is achieved quickly. That's not to say it's never good to tell someone directly what to do with their body or to put them in a particular position in the swing, I just prefer to avoid tying people in knots.

Most of us who teach the game for a living started out as aspiring competitive players. I'll never know what it feels like to win the Masters, but I can honestly tell you it is very satisfying and rewarding to hear from a student who just won the Club Championship or broke 90 for the first time. I get to share the glory with hundreds of people, the recreational players, the people who make up the heart and soul of golf. Not a bad way to make a living, is it?

Hopefully this book will give you the necessary tools to make your goals a little easier to attain. Will it cure your game? I doubt it. If all the books, videos and gadgets out there did what they claim, the average score for 18 holes would be 18! Will you pick up a few tips that might knock a couple strokes off? I certainly hope so!

ATTENTION LEFT HANDERS

Sorry to inform you this book has been written as if speaking to right handed players. They account for over 90% of all golfers, and it would be too confusing to try to write this in both left and right handed terminology. I speak both languages, I just can't write them! Hope you can follow along anyway.

I. SHORT GAME

The short game consists of any shot requiring less than a full swing. It is used mostly on and around the green but there are other situations such has escaping from trees, where short game techniques are utilized. It accounts for a majority of all shots yet most amateurs practice it the least.

There is no way to put a value on a good short game. Some of my best scoring rounds have featured mediocre ball striking but spectacular chipping and putting.

A good short game gives you confidence and takes pressure off your long game.

We always start our golf schools with putting and move up from there. That's where the title of this book, "Golf From the Ground Up," was derived. It's not intended to be some world stopping, high - tech teaching method, it's just a sequence that most students find sensible and easy to follow.

Establishing good short game skills prepares our students to make the transition to the long game. It's like building a house. You don't start with the roof and work down. You construct a solid foundation on which to assemble your structure.

When you watch golf highlights on TV, almost all the shots they show are short ones. As fun as it is to launch the ball a mile, there is not a more exhilarating feeling as sinking a long, important putt or chipping in from off the green.

Practice your short game diligently. You'll reap tremendous rewards.

PUTTING

I like to think of the putting stroke as a miniature golf swing and the golf swing as a giant putting stroke. Putting accounts for over 40% of your score. In short, improved putting produces lower scores.

The basic requirement is to contact the ball on the sweet spot of a putter face that is square to your intended line and with the proper amount of speed. Sounds simple enough but there are some key elements that help you get the job done consistently.

Let's start by identifying the true "sweet spot" on your putter. It isn't always where the manufacturer has put the line. As shown in the picture, hold your club very gently just below the grip with your thumb and index finger. Take the pointed end of a tee and tap on the clubface till you find the point that resists twisting. If this point is not where the manufacturer has indicated, you may want to mark this spot with a dab of paint or scribe a small line with a hacksaw. **Solid contact is often taken for granted in putting but is a key ingredient toward developing consistency.**

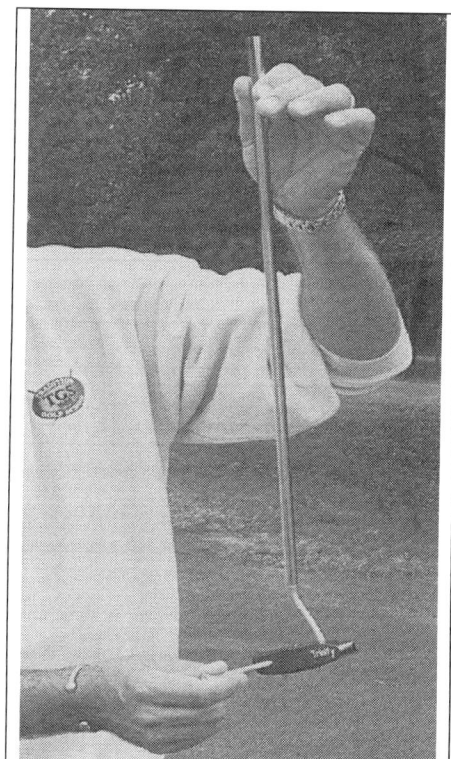

It's easy to find the sweet spot or *center of gravity* on the putter face by holding the putter very gently on the shaft, right below the grip and tapping the face till you find the spot that resists twisting. In this case I'm using a tee but you can use the scorecard pencil or even the end of your finger. Practice a few putts with masking tape on the putter face and look to see where you're making contact.

Missing the sweet spot by just a fraction of an inch can adversely affect both distance and direction.

THE KILLER MOVE

The most common putting error we see (beside a bad haircut!) is pictured to the left. **The Dreaded Flip!** Let's figure out what's wrong with this picture. Take a look at the left arm, most notably the wrist. See the giant crease in the wrist? This is a classic case of the club head passing the hands due to excessive wrist action. At this point in the follow through, the club shaft and left arm should be forming a straight line. The left wrist should be flat and the right wrist should be creased. As you can see the wrists are exactly opposite that position. In addition, the arms should be forming a **"TRIANGLE"** or **"V."** We call this **"Flipping" at it**. One of the reasons we begin with putting is to tackle this problem right from the start. This same move has been known to rear its ugly head in other golf shots too.

Kids: Do not try this at home. The **KILLER MOVE** leads to dangerously high scores!

This above position would actually be pretty good if the player were putting left handed! But don't fret; the **KILLER MOVE** afflicts even the greatest of players, which is why we see so many different styles on television. This chapter will explain how to conquer the **KILLER MOVE** and lead you on a path to consistency.

Imagine a paintbrush on the end of the shaft and "paint" a smooth stripe on the green. Notice that the handle of the brush leads the bristles and the shaft is in a line with the left arm. If the bristles flip past the handle you'll perform the **KILLER MOVE** and splatter paint everywhere.

Here are a few techniques that have become popular. *While a vast majority of players hold the club conventionally, don't be afraid to experiment* a bit and learn what works best for you. Remember all these different styles were adopted primarily in an effort to avoid the **KILLER MOVE**. The Mr. T starter kit (jewelry) is optional.

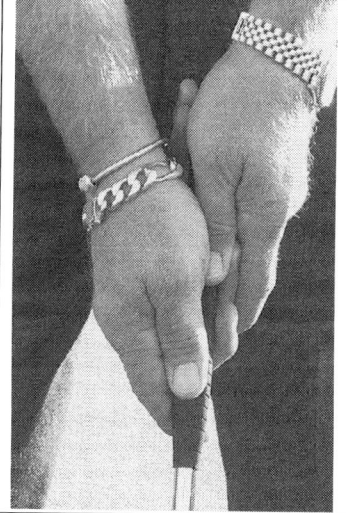	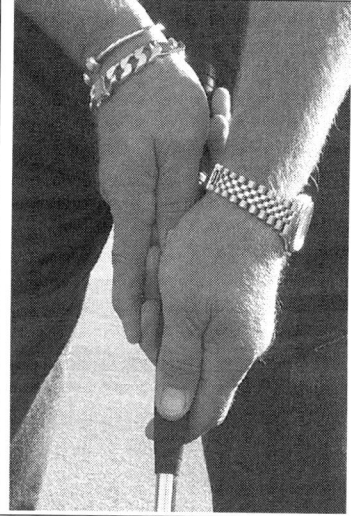	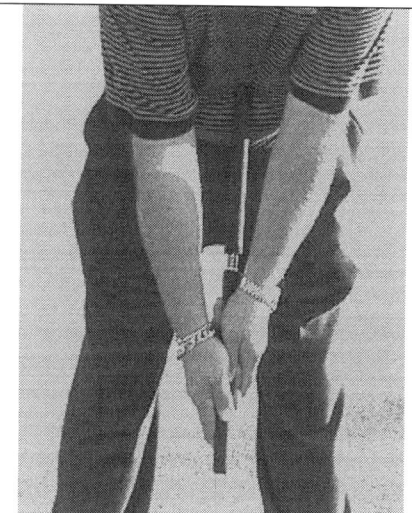
Conventional *Reverse Overlap* Notice how the left index finger overlaps the right little finger.	**Cross-handed** or *Left Hand Low*. Aligns the club with left arm and creates larger crease in right wrist.	*Belly Putter* Grip cap actually touches the belly and stays there throughout stroke. Easy to maintain triangle this way.
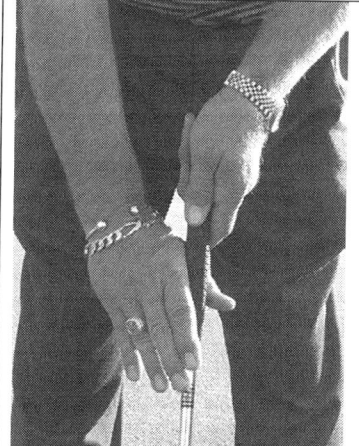	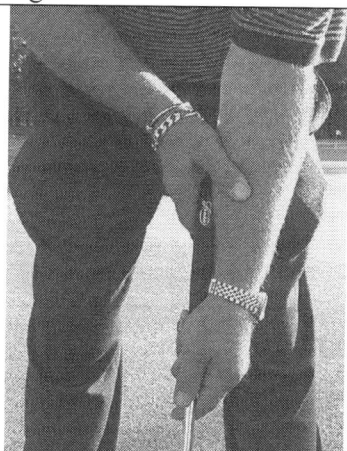	
The Claw Allows hands to stay passive and soft on club. Works well on fast greens.	*The Splint* Handle of club is braced inside left forearm and held there by right hand.	*Long Putter* Club rests against sternum for true pendulum effect. Some have even rested their chin on grip cap of club!

There's no right or wrong. Whatever works for you is what's suggested.

GETTING STARTED

Now that you've identified the sweet spot on your putter and chosen a way to hold the club, let's put our plan into action. For the remainder of this chapter, we'll assume you're holding the club conventionally. If not, these recommendations will still be easy to adapt to your own style.

THE TRIANGLE

When addressing the ball, we like to see the arms form a **TRIANGLE** or "**V**" which means the arms need to be fully extended but not locked straight. ***This is accomplished by bending mostly from the hips so the arms have plenty of room to hang naturally.*** You may find that your putter is too long for you to get into this position without gripping way down toward the bottom of the handle. This is perfectly acceptable however; if the handle is too close to your body, consider having your putter shortened. This is a simple process which should only cost a few dollars at a repair shop.

Address	Backswing	Follow Through
Notice the **TRIANGLE** formed by the arms at address. Also note that the handle is a little closer to the target than the club head and the ball is positioned a little forward (left) of center in the stance.	The head and body stay still while the **TRIANGLE** stays intact. The gap between the wrists hasn't changed from address. Your weight should start and remain fairly evenly distributed throughout the stroke.	Again, the head and body remain motionless while the **V** or **TRIANGLE** is still intact. The arms, shoulders and club are working as a single unit. Note the shaft is still in line with the left arm.

> You may benefit from practicing without a club by forming your **TRIANGLE** and pressing your palms flat together. Now stand as still as possible and move only the **TRIANGLE** back and forth.

DISTANCE FROM BALL

It is generally accepted that the best place to position the eyes is directly over the golf ball. By so doing, you'll get the best view of the line you want the ball to travel on and have a much better chance of aiming properly. This is another situation that may cause you to realize your putter is too long for you.

Eyes Inside the Line
Standing too far away positions your eyes between your feet and the ball. The hole will appear to be more to the right than it is and you'll tend to take the club head back to the inside or toward your body.

Eyes Over the Line/ Ball
From here you have your best chance for aiming properly and executing a straight back and through stroke.
Note most of the bending is at the hips and the weight is on the balls of the feet, under the shoelaces.

Eyes Outside the Line
If your eyes are positioned too far outside the golf ball, the hole will appear more to the left than it is and you will tend to take your backswing to the outside (away from your body) because your arms won't have enough room to swing straight back.

EXECUTING THE STROKE

Now that you're armed with all this information, let's try to sink some putts. In our golf schools, we teach the stroke backwards; meaning we start with the follow through and add the backswing later.

No Backswing?

Starting no more than 2 feet from the hole, get into your address position and put the putter face up against the back of the ball. From here, simply push the ball to the hole keeping the ball on the clubface. The club head should stay low and the face should remain square to the target. Most importantly, your arms should remain in the **V** or **TRIANGLE**. Hold your finish and look to see if you've accomplished this. Your hands, wrists, arms and putter should still be in the same position in which they began.

This is not a legal stroke but it is a great drill for emphasizing follow through and a good step toward eliminating the **KILLER MOVE.**

Continue doing this from about 4 feet until you're making most every putt. Keep in mind that from four feet, the putter won't go all the way through to the hole.

Now let's add some back swing to the stroke. At this close range, you won't need to go back very far at all. In fact a good frame of reference is to ***think 1/3 backswing, 2/3 follow through.*** Even though most textbooks will tell you to have an even stroke, I think it's best to put a little more emphasis on the follow through. This is to encourage an accelerating stroke and to discourage "hitting at" the ball.

Following are some key elements to good putting:
- Relax, Relax, Relax. It starts with the shoulders. The arms should hang naturally and feel very light.
- Soft Grip Pressure.
- Steady Head. If the head stays steady, so will the body.
- Listen for the ball to drop in the cup, don't look.
- Rhythm. Think "Tick – Tock" not "Flip – Flop!" The ball just gets in the way.
- Your body should act like a grandfather clock. The shoulders, arms, wrists and club are the pendulum; working as a single unit. The **TRIANGLE!!**

AIMING

Oh yeah, we have to aim at something too, don't we? Almost everyone has trouble with alignment but it shouldn't be that difficult. Most of the time we just neglect to pay careful attention to where we are aimed. To be able to aim properly you need to understand the "Railroad Track" analogy and what "Parallel Left" means.

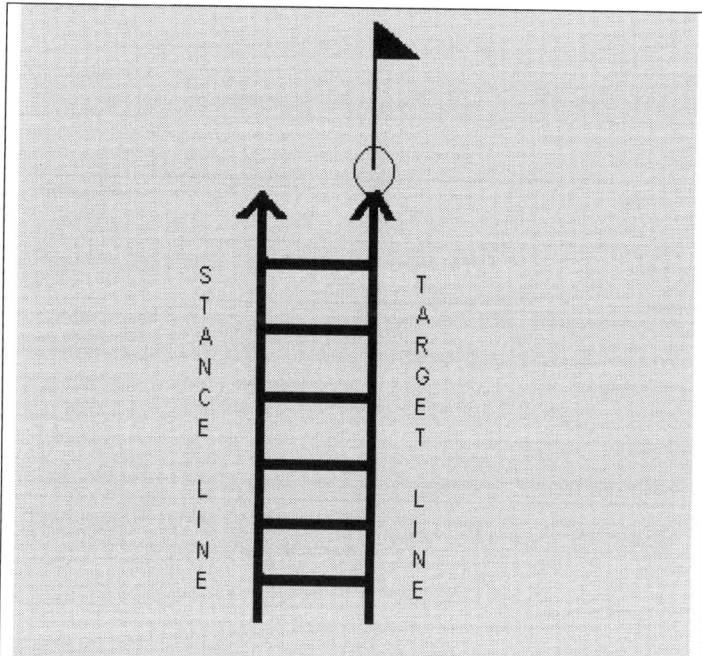

This diagram illustrates the proper way to align for almost all golf shots. The club and ball should be on the target line, the feet, knees, hips and shoulders will be on the stance line; parallel to, but left of, the target line. Hence the railroad track image.

You may want to use a trainer like the one above to help you line up properly. This one is marked at various intervals to help measure backswing and follow through. Two clubs or dowels will work too.

Okay, got it? Now let's try to read the green and see if the putt will break or curve. We also need to establish a routine so we're sure to be doing the same thing each time.

Reading the greens is somewhat of an art. No matter how long you've been playing, there will still be some guesswork involved. For the most part, you want to focus on the last few feet of the putt because ***90% of the break usually occurs during the last 10% of the putt***. This is when gravity begins to overtake momentum, assuming the ball is rolling at the proper speed. (Don't worry; we'll cover that speed thing pretty soon.) Here are a few basic tips for reading the greens.

- Get a good look at the green from the fairway. 30 to 40 yards away is your best bet. Picture water draining from the green and look at the overall contour.
- Don't overanalyze. Looking at the putt from every angle will likely confuse you and make you wonder why your friends don't call you to play golf anymore.
- Take a quick peek from the back of the hole, preferably on your way to your golf ball, as you approach the green. While walking to your ball from the hole, take note through your feet as to whether you're walking uphill, side- hill or downhill.
- From behind the ball, in a crouched position, look to see if there is a low or high side to the cup. The ball will break toward the low side.
- Picture water being poured in front of the cup. Which way will it drain? The ball will go in the direction of drainage.
- If the grass looks dark, you're into the grain. (slower) A lighter shinier look to the grass means you're down grain and the putt will be faster. You may very well have a 'multi grain" putt at times.
- Look for the "ragged edge" on the rim of the cup. The grain is growing toward it.

This is the best place from which to read a putt.	Always line up the club first…..	…then step in to finish your stance and grip.

Notice the dark spot on the green a couple feet in front of the ball? That's called an **intermediate target**. Having already read the putt, I know if I can start the ball over that spot, it will be on the right line. Some people like to aim the brand name of the ball or draw a stripe on it with a magic marker and align the stripe to the line.	This putt breaks a lot from right to left. It's hard to see my intermediate target but in this case, I'm aiming a little to the right of it. (You can't always find a target exactly on your line.) I'm trying to putt this ball to the other ball in the picture. From there the slope of the green should take it to the hole. This is called **segment putting.**

So far we've talked about technique and aiming, but we haven't addressed the most difficult aspect of putting; *distance control*. Take a look at how you and others putt. You'll see that most of the time your distance is worse than your aim. Why is this? Because most of direction is taken care of before we even execute the stroke. Distance control is almost all "feel" and requires a tremendous amount of practice. Not only are you constantly confronted with different length putts, some are downhill, uphill and across the hill, each requiring a different touch. Then of course, there's the green speed that varies from course to course. Unfortunately, there is no substitute for practice but that doesn't mean there aren't a few drills you can do to improve.

- *Practice with one ball*. You play golf with only one ball, don't you? Using one ball and going from hole to hole is a great way to mix it up and not just putt the same putt over and over again. It makes practice more like playing. If you can find a playing partner who likes a friendly wager, it will make things more fun and help you learn to concentrate.

- *Putt with your eyes closed*. Seriously; that's not a typo. Go through your entire setup routine, and then close your eyes before you make the stroke. Picture in your mind the distance from the ball to the hole.

- *Look at the hole while you putt*. Similar to the last drill but look at the hole instead of the ball. A good way to build in feel.

- *The Par 6 Drill*. Place three balls on the same line at 6, 12 and 18 feet. Start with the closest ball and try to sink all 3 in no more than a total of 6 putts. Experienced players should try for 3 putts. Change angles and distances frequently.

- *Putt one handed*. Try your right hand first. Think of the shaft as an extension of your arm and the clubface as the palm of your hand. Try to envision that you are rolling the ball underhanded with your extra long arm. Note how freely you stroke through the ball and that you don't flip your wrist. Left handed works well too especially for getting the feel for keeping the left wrist firm through contact avoiding the **KILLER MOVE**.

- ***Putt to edge of green***. Drop a few balls in the center of the green and see how close you can putt to the edge of the green without going off the green.

- ***Get the ball to the hole***. I try to roll my putts fast enough so that if they miss, they go about 1 foot past the cup. Obviously they need to have enough speed to get to the hole, but running it 6 feet past is not much better than leaving it 6 feet short. The only advantage is you can watch the ball roll past the cup and get a good read for the putt coming back.

- ***Putt with a stripe on the ball***. Usually a range ball will do or draw a stripe on one of your own golf balls. Line up the stripe in the direction you want the ball to roll. If you contact the ball squarely, the stripe will remain visible throughout the roll. If you miss – hit, the stripe will barely be visible. By making consistent contact, it will be easier to judge how hard to contact the ball.

- ***Use the same kind of ball***. It doesn't really matter which ball you prefer but it does make sense to use the same kind of ball all the time. Some balls are harder than others and come off the clubface a little faster. Find out if you prefer a softer or harder feel and stick with it.

You're probably clever enough to come up with some drills of your own too. Here are a few I've been known to practice.

The cup reducer. Place 2 tees about 3 inches apart in front of the cup and try putting your ball between the tees. This helps you focus on the center of the cup and trains you to putt to a smaller target.	Tuck a long club under your arms and you'll get a good sensation of an arm & shoulder motion. The club should rock up and down, not twist sideways.	A pen, tongue depressor, even a comb can make a great "splint" for your left wrist. Remember you can't do this while playing; only practicing!

- ***The Clock face.*** My nemesis has always been 3 footers. Too far away for a tap – in, too close to not make. With the hole as the center of the clock face, start at the 1 o'clock position, 3 feet away and work your way around to 12 o'clock. Don't stop till you've made all 12 in a row. If you miss one, sorry, it's 1 o'clock again!

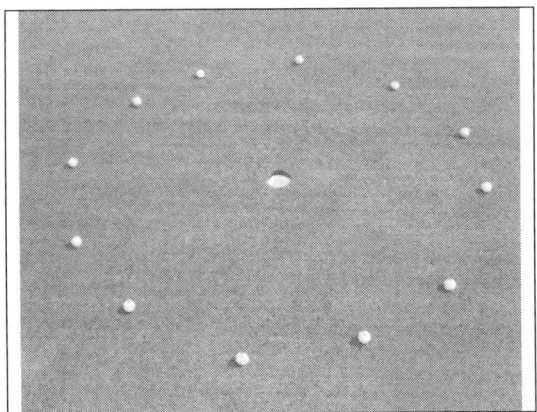

TEACHING AIDS

We use an assortment of teaching aids in our golf school. Some we make ourselves, others we purchase the same way you would.

The Kure
This device attaches to the front of the shaft and fits between the forearms. It is a very effective way to retain the **TRIANGLE** and combat the **KILLER MOVE**. You can capture the same feel by putting something like a large sponge, roll of paper towels or soccer ball between your arms.

This is a device we manufacture ourselves called the "Stroke Straightener." It rests on the ground and guides your stroke by forcing the putter head to stay between the lines. Note the "ruler" for gauging the length of the stroke.

- Every time you putt the ball, your goal should be to *make* the putt. That sounds incredibly obvious but most people don't expect to sink the putt, they just hope the ball will end up somewhere near the hole. With a positive "I can make this" approach, you'll eventually convince yourself that you are a good putter and you'll actually make more putts.

- Despite your efforts to be positive, don't be disappointed if every putt doesn't drop. On average, a PGA tour player is more likely to miss a putt from 6 feet than he is to make it.

Before we close this chapter, let's talk a little bit about the putter you are using. Your putter is the most used club in the bag yet often the most neglected. It is important you have a putter that truly fits. We use a putter fitting system that factors in your vision (eye dominance, near sightedness, etc,) as well as your physical makeup. We even use a laser to show you how to aim. If you know of a good putter fitter in your area, it's worth the time to find out if the putter you're currently using is right for you.

Some of the specifications we consider when fitting a putter include:
- Length
- Lie angle
- Grip size
- Grip material
- Weight
- Club head material
- Cosmetics
- Clubface material
- Offset
- Shaft material
- Loft

Never underestimate the value of being a good putter. It takes pressure off your long game and can really frustrate your opponents. You can score well on days when you're not contacting the ball solidly, but no one can score well without good putting.

Now, let's go chip!

CHIPPING

The chip shot is described as a low, running shot that is usually performed from very near the edge of the green. It is a valuable shot to have and also serves as a primer for learning to make solid contact in the iron game. The technique does not change much from putting; the biggest changes take place in the setup.

An example of a chip shot is pictured here. The ball is a few feet from the edge of the green and the hole is about 60 feet away. The object is to produce a shot with a low trajectory that lands in the circle, about 15 feet away, and rolls the rest of the way. ***There is no need for a high, soft shot here because the only obstacle that needs to be carried is the grass between the ball and the edge of the green.*** Try this shot with a variety of clubs to determine your carry to roll ratios with each club then stay with the one that feels most comfortable.

Before we discuss technique, let's talk club selection. In nearly all chipping situations, it is best to **use the least amount of loft the shot will allow**. We usually teach with an 8 iron but if a putter will work, that will likely be your best choice. Not that you should plan to fail but, just in case, a poor shot with a putter is usually better than a poor shot with an iron. Otherwise, choose the club that enables you to land the ball on the edge of the green and roll it to the cup. ***It is much easier to roll the ball to the cup than it is to carry it there.***

This is also the point where we need to determine how we plan to hold the club. Each player will hold the club a little differently but there are some basic guidelines we can all follow.

- Grip pressure should be soft enough to maintain good feel but firm enough to maintain a constant grip on the club. About a 6 on a scale of 10.
- Hands should be close together to encourage working as one.
- Palms should oppose one another.
- Left thumb should fit into lifeline of right hand.
- Overall grip is more in fingers than palms.

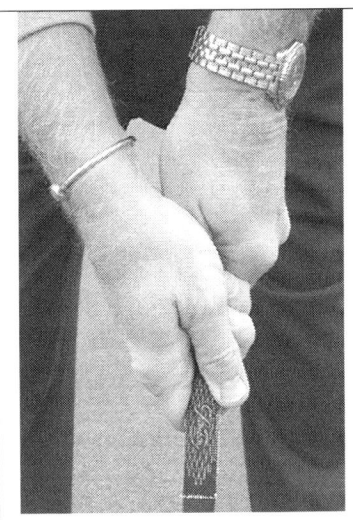	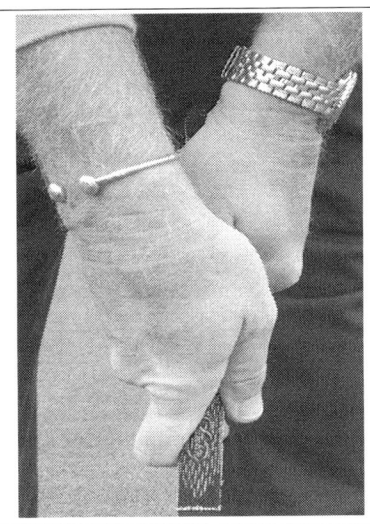	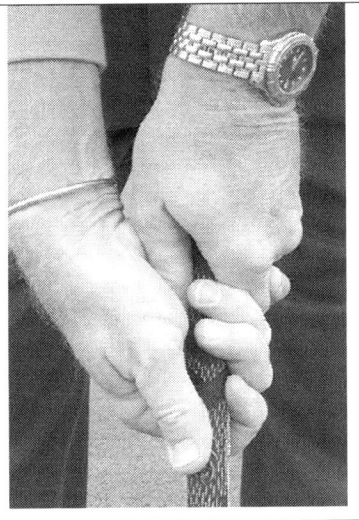
This would be considered a good, conventional grip. Notice the "V's" formed by the thumb and index fingers. Both point toward the right shoulder.	When the V's point to the player's left, it encourages an open clubface and is considered a "weak" grip.	A "strong" grip occurs when the player turns his hands clockwise on the handle and the V's point well right. This will promote a closed clubface.
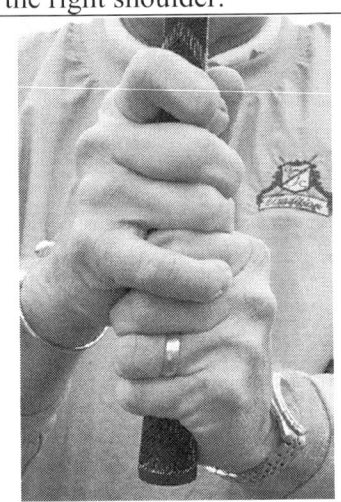	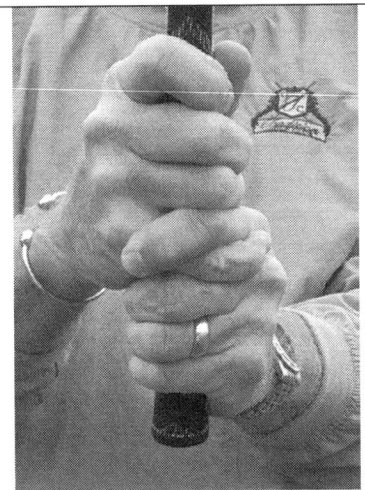	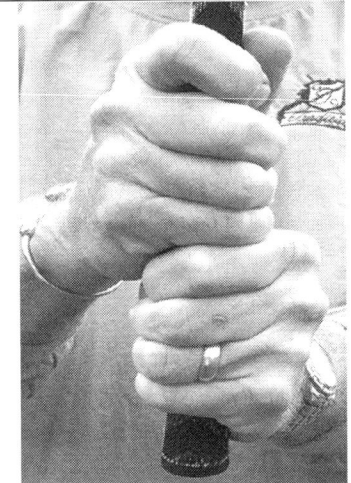
When the right little finger overlaps the left index, it is called an overlapping or "Vardon" grip.	Here the same two fingers form the "interlocking" grip.	This is the ten finger or "baseball" grip. Make sure your hands stay close together if using this grip.

- Find the grip that works best for you and stick with it. Make sure you have a fundamentally sound grip. It's the hinge between you and your club and will affect how you swing. ***If you don't start with a good grip, it is very difficult to change it later.***

Okay, back to chipping……………..

Setup	Backswing	Contact	Follow Through

Grip down a little. Narrow stance. Open stance. Ball centered. 2/3 of weight left. Handle forward.	• Body still. • Hands quiet. • Maintain **TRIANGLE**.	• Nearly same as address. • A little bit of right knee starting to kick in.	• Club head low. • Right knee toward target. • **TRIANGLE** intact. • Left wrist firm.

The feel of the chipping stroke is similar to putting in that the wrists remain quiet and the **TRIANGLE** stays intact. The differences are the backswing will come up a little so we can contact the ball on the downswing and we'll add a little lower body or **PIVOT** on the follow through. You'll read a lot more about the **PIVOT** as we continue to longer shots.

To acquire the image of contacting the ball on the downswing, ***imagine a large jetliner coming in for a smooth landing***. There is a slightly descending approach, then a shallow or level landing. The narrow stance is for comfort because we don't have to swing hard. The open stance is to encourage a straight backswing and to pre-set a little room for the follow through. The weight favors the left side to help anchor the body and encourage taking the club back a little steeper than a putting stroke. This will set up the descending angle back to the ball.

- ***In general, the stance will be open (left foot pulled back) and narrow when ever the shot requires less than a full swing.***

| I'm baaaack!! Oh no the **KILLER MOVE** has returned to invade our chipping game. Is there any stopping it? When using irons, many weekend players contact the ball with the shaft leaning away from the target as if trying to scoop the ball into the air. | Experienced players will contact the ball on the downswing with the shaft leaning toward the target. This allows the leading edge of the clubface to easily slide under the ball, resulting in clean, crisp contact. Hey, haven't we seen that **TRIANGLE** somewhere before? |

When a player applies the **KILLER MOVE** to a chip shot, he will either contact the ground behind the ball (chunk it) or, more likely, "blade" the ball by contacting it near its equator with the bottom of the club. This shot usually goes screaming to the other side of the green. After which the player is accused of having topped the ball because he "looked up." Believe it or not, looking up rarely happens. What *does* happen is *swinging up;* a sub conscious effort to lift the ball into the air; yet another example of the, you guessed it, **KILLER MOVE**.

Here are a few ideas and drills to help you visualize and feel a properly executed chip shot.

This club has a glass strapped to the shaft. Imagine the glass being filled with water, then try not to spill any.

Apply the **KILLER MOVE** here and you'll have water, water everywhere!

Torture Club
This club has an extra long shaft. Notice that because my left wrist and elbow are bent, the shaft has hit me in the left side. If my arms were still in the **TRIANGLE**, the shaft would have cleared my left side and my ribs wouldn't hurt.

This is not a pretty picture but we see it all the time in our golf schools. Here I've lost a tough battle with the **KILLER MOVE.** My elbows are very far apart and the left arm has formed the infamous *chicken wing*.

- Try a few shots with only your right hand on the club. Sense that you are simply tossing the ball underhanded with your golf club. Notice how your lower body helps just a little. Now apply that sensation with both hands on the club.

CHIP UNDER A BENCH

For crisp contact, envision chipping the ball under a bench or coffee table.

HOLD YOUR FINISH

Notice that after the ball has been contacted the club head is well underneath the hands and also to the outside, or right of the hands. If you can nail this finish, you'll make solid contact with the golf ball.

JUMP THROUGH A HOOP

This may look goofy but believe me, this is a very effective drill to learn how to chip. The hoop is about 4 feet in front of the golf ball. My job is to chip the ball through the hoop. In order to do so, the club will follow through low and the wrists will remain firm.

PITCHING

Opposite of a chip, the pitch shot spends most of its time in the air and rolls less than it carries. The trajectory resembles that of a pitch thrown in slow pitch softball. Usually performed with a wedge, pitch shots come in many shapes and forms and require a good deal of skill, finesse, creativity, touch and **PRACTICE**. This is arguably the most important part of the game, yet one of the least practiced by weekend players.

Here's an example of when a pitch shot would be needed; about 30 yards over a bunker with 10 feet of green between the hole and the edge of the bunker. The ball will need to fly high and land softly to get close to the hole. There are a number of ways to execute this shot but this chapter will focus primarily on one technique. *Do try to practice these shots as much as possible using the various wedges in your bag. These are the shots that will reveal the artist in you!*

As we expand our swing to execute a pitch shot, we need to involve a few more body parts which tend to complicate things. This is where we learn to **PIVOT**; the rotation of the body toward the target on the follow through. A **PIVOT** is necessary to provide room for our arms on the follow through and to give us a little extra power to carry the ball farther. It has been said that the **PIVOT** is the engine of the golf swing. We make similar motions when throwing a ball, swinging a racquet or baseball bat. The difference is we do it in a reactionary manner with relaxed muscles, whereas in golf we start from a standstill, often with tension filled muscles.

The single most important ingredient is solid contact. You can miss – hit a wood or iron and still get away with a decent shot. A miss – hit with the wedge usually adds more than one stroke to the score. To make solid contact, the leading edge (bottom line on the clubface) must find its way under the ball. To do so, the club must be traveling downward as it contacts the ball. Any attempt to lift or scoop the ball will result in the **KILLER MOVE**. You'll either contact the ground behind the ball or worse yet, the middle of the ball with the bottom of the club. This will send the ball screaming along the ground, completely out of control.

SETUP	TAKEAWAY	CONTACT	FOLLOW THROUGH
• Weight left. • Hands left. • Stance open and fairly narrow. • Ball centered.	• Body still. • Left arm and shaft form an "L" as the wrists cock.	• Right knee toward target. • Shaft leaning forward. • **TRIANGLE.**	• Body rotated. • Arms still in **TRIANGLE.** • Very little weight on right side.

Note: You may not need to cock the wrists this much. It depends on the lie and how far you want the ball to go. Read on!

- Ball position is related to the type of lie you have and the required trajectory. Generally, the worse the lie is, the more you need to play the ball back in your stance.

- If you have a good lie with the ball sitting atop the grass, you can probably use a stroke similar to a chip or a putt; very little wrist action.

- If the lie is poor, such as in deep grass or a divot, you will probably need to cock your wrists a little on the backswing to establish a steeper angle toward the ball. This is to ensure the leading edge of the club gets under the ball.

- To fly the ball higher, play the ball more toward the left (forward) side of your stance. Make sure you have a good lie. There's a higher risk of blading the ball when playing it forward.

- Playing the ball toward the right (back) side of the stance will fly the ball lower.

Here are two images that may help you execute a pitch shot.

1. Imagine turning to shake hands with someone. Notice that the lower body initiates the turn.

2. You'll sense the same feeling when throwing a ball underhanded. Guess that's why they call it a pitch shot!

Another good way to coordinate the body and arms is to try this drill.

With the club in your right hand, grab your right pocket with your left hand and start your downswing by pulling the pocket.

This will teach you to lead with your lower body and swing smoothly.

Follow through to a balanced finish. Congratulations. You just learned how to **PIVOT!**

Envision the club head as if it is swinging like a child on a swing at the playground.

MORE PITCHING TIPS

See the line across my toes? That's the **"roadmap"** for the golf swing. Make sure your club swings back over that line.

If you go back way to the "inside" as I have here, you'll come in from too shallow an approach and blade, chunk or shank a lot of shots.

Make sure you finish the swing by **PIVOTING**. The fact that the arms are hidden indicates they're still in front of the body, just like at address.

Uh oh. Here the wrists have flipped the club head. **(KILLER MOVE)** The shaft should still be in line with the left arm but it's actually more in line with the right arm. Usually this will produce a bladed shot.

THE KILLER MOVE FROM THE BACK SIDE

The "flip" is evident here as the hands are still in front of the body and the shaft is pointing up.

Here the **TRIANGLE** is intact, the hands have swung past the body and the club shaft is still in line with the left arm.

A time honored method for distance control is pictured below. Imagine yourself standing in a clock face with 12:00 o'clock above your head and 6 o'clock at your feet.

Here's a short pitch. My thumbs point to 8 o'clock on the back swing. Very little wrist action. Much like a chip.	On the follow through the thumbs point to 4 o'clock and the arms are still in the **TRIANGLE**. Note a hint of **PIVOT** here.

A longer swing points to 9 o'clock with a little bit of wrist cock.	A 3 o'clock finish requires a little more **PIVOT.** The arms are still in the **TRIANGLE.**

To point to 10 o'clock, make an **"L"** with your left arm and club. Think "Thumbs Up."	Here's a "REVERSE L" pointing at 2 o'clock. This would be for an even longer shot.

NONE, NONE, NONE. SOME, NONE, NONE. SOME, NONE, SOME.

What the heck am I talking about? Have I totally lost it? Actually this is a neat way to remember when and where to apply wrist action in the short game. I wish I thought of this myself but I must give credit to Craig Shankland, one of the top instructors in the country.

No wrist action has been used. Handle points at belly. **NONE**	Again, no wrists. Handle points at belly. **NONE**	No wrists here either. Handle points at belly. **NONE**

Notice the wrists and elbows stay the same distance apart throughout the stroke. This is a very safe method because there are few moving parts. The **TRIANGLE** stays intact. This technique is also considered a "One Lever" system. Use this shot for chips and short pitches, particularly when the lie is good.

For a little longer distance utilizing "NONE, NONE, NONE," complete the **PIVOT** of the body so the **TRIANGLE** points toward the target. In this case my arms have not moved independently. They've simply hitched a ride on the **PIVOT** and are still in the address position. Basically I've turned my address or starting position 90° to my left. Although my arm extension might be a bit exaggerated, if you have trouble making solid contact with your wedges, you should endeavor to finish like this.

| The wrists have cocked to establish the angle required to contact the ball on the downswing. **SOME** | Still no wrists here. **NONE** | Or here. **NONE** |

Use this shot when the ball is sitting down or in deeper grass. You'll probably use this shot the most for little wedge shots near the green.

| Wrists are cocked here….. **SOME** | …but not here. Are you seeing a pattern? **NONE** | Wrists have un-cocked here. **SOME** |

This shot comes in handy for longer pitches requiring a little more club speed. Because of the speed, the body turns through and the wrists "release" a little more. **Note there's always "NONE" at impact.**

II. FULL SWING

You've already built the foundation for your full swing by working on your short game. Now we'll increase the size of the swing; altering the set up and turning the body a bit more. Before we get into that, let's talk about some of the fundamentals and terminology.

FUNDAMENTALS

- **GRIP.** Continue using the same grip you chose in the chipping chapter.
- **ALIGNMENT.** This is probably the most abused fundamental in golf. In fact 85% of right handed players aim to the right of the target. This is because the tendency is to aim the body at the target which places the club well to the right. Remember the railroad track image we discussed in putting? The exact same technique applies to the full swing as well. Get in the habit of aligning your clubface to the target first, use an intermediate target if necessary, then align your body parallel but left of the target line. ***Remember, the club aims at the target, the body aims left of the target. This is extremely important because if you are not aligned properly you'll have to make some sort of mid swing adjustment to make the ball go to the target.***
- **POSTURE.** You can follow these easy steps to find proper posture and distance from the ball for every club in the bag.

Hold your club in front of you about waist high. Your arms should form the **TRIANGLE** with the upper part of the arms staying close to your chest.			Bend from the hips and let the club drop to the ground. The knees will be slightly flexed for comfort. Most of your weight on the balls of the feet, under the shoelaces.

The shaft is perpendicular to the spine with about **a hand span between the butt end of the club and your body**. Your arms should hang freely and feel very light. It is very important to **maintain your posture and spine angle throughout the swing.** Notice the back of the belt is higher than the front.

- **STANCE WIDTH.** It varies a bit from player to player. A tall person may require a wide stance for balance but too wide can restrict the **PIVOT.** A good starting point is to align the outsides of the feet with the outsides of the shoulders. Turning the left foot toward the target a little helps you make a better **PIVOT** and is less strenuous on the back.

- **BALL POSITION.** This also varies among players due to eye dominance, range of motion and swing styles. Generally, the ball should be positioned about in the center of the stance for wedges, a little left of center for short and mid irons, a little farther left for long irons and fairway woods and just opposite the inside of the left foot for tee shots. When using an iron from a tee, play the ball a little more forward (left) than you normally would. *There is no need to position the ball right of center for any full swing shot. That side of the stance is for the short game and specialty shots which we'll discuss later.*

- **WEIGHT DISTRIBUTION.** During the short game we kept our weight to our left side because we wanted a steep backswing and we were trying to stay very still on the backswing. For the full swing, your weight is evenly distributed and gradually moves a little toward the right side as you work your way up to the driver.

Your swing should not consciously change from club to club but your setup will a little. *The only things that will change are ball position and weight distribution.* Your distance from the ball changes too, but that happens automatically due to the varying lengths of the clubs.	Notice here the grip end of the club is about the same distance from the body with the driver, mid iron and wedge. Allow approximately a hand span between your body and club.

Sometimes the results are remarkable when one learns the proper weight distribution for the setup; especially for tee shots.

For wedges play the ball in the middle of your stance with your weight slightly favoring the left side and the shaft leaning toward the target.	For irons the stance will widen somewhat and the ball should be forward of center or opposite the left side of your face. The shaft should still lean toward the target and your weight will slightly favor the right side.	Fairway woods should still be swung in a manner that allows contact with the ball on the downswing. I like to take a divot with a fairway wood. However, too steep an attack angle will destroy any chances to get the ball airborne. Position the ball left of center but set up a little more on your right side.	To drive the ball, contact should be made past the bottom of the club's arc and actually slightly on the upswing. I like to think of a jetliner just lifting its nose wheel on its takeoff roll. To promote this type of swing, position the ball opposite the left instep and really tilt your spine away from the target. Your left shoulder will be considerably farther from the target than your left hip. Tee the ball as high as you comfortably can.

A simple way to remember correct weight distribution when addressing the ball is ***the closer the ball is to the green, the closer your weight should be to the green and the farther your ball is from the green the farther your weight should be too.***

THE ALIGNER

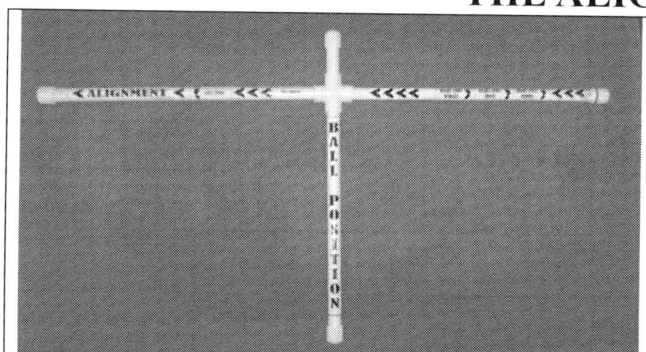

This is another device we make for alignment and ball position. The longer tube is for aiming and the shorter tube slides back and forth for ball position. It even has markings for left and right foot positions for each club. Call now. Operators are standing by!

BALL FLIGHT LAWS

Oh boy, this is going to be exciting! According to the PGA Teaching Manual, ball flight laws "rank as the first priority because they are absolute rather than arbitrary. They work every time without fail." In other words, an understanding of the physics behind ball flight provides a clear image of why shots go where they go.

Let's start with the most obvious ball flight law, **SOLID CONTACT.** No matter how pretty a swing may look, it is useless if the ball is not struck squarely on the clubface. You can tap the face of an iron in the same manner in which we tapped the putter face. You may be surprised to find the sweet spot is a little closer to the heel of the club in the irons and therefore not in the measured center of the face. You may want to mark an iron face with a magic marker to help you zero in on the exact spot where you want to make contact. Do the same with your woods. For the most part, you'll want to try to contact the ball on the exact center of the face with the woods.

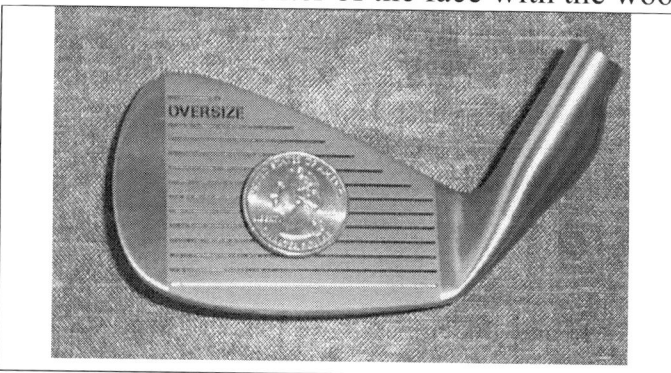

The **CLUBFACE ANGLE** has the biggest influence on direction.

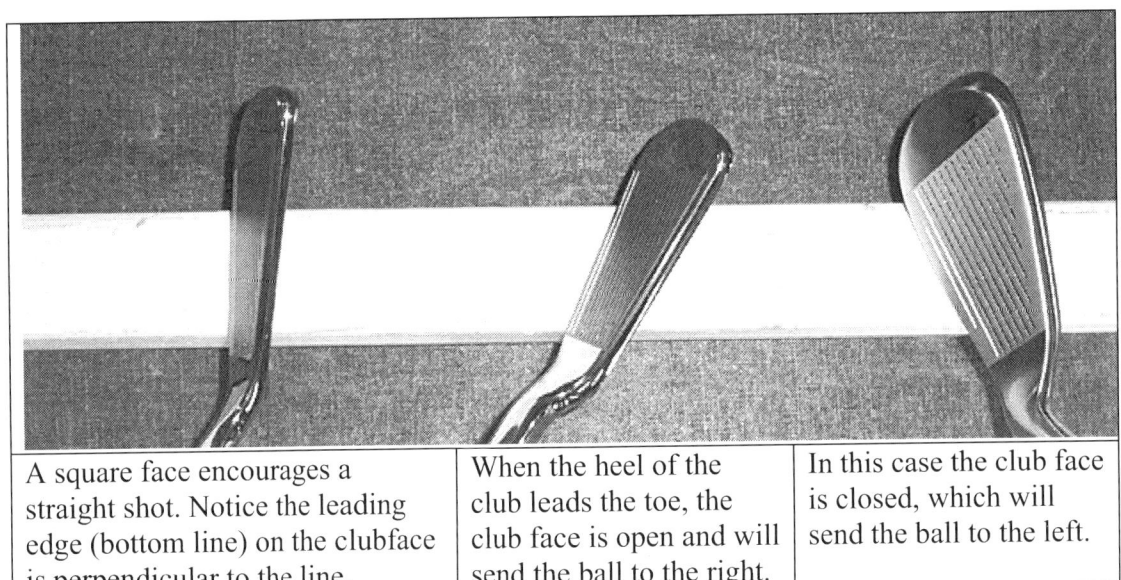

| A square face encourages a straight shot. Notice the leading edge (bottom line) on the clubface is perpendicular to the line. | When the heel of the club leads the toe, the club face is open and will send the ball to the right. | In this case the club face is closed, which will send the ball to the left. |

The **SWING PATH** is the direction the club head travels through impact relative to the target line. It will influence the *initial* direction of a shot. *Assuming solid contact, the swing path and clubface angle combine to determine the shape of your shots.*

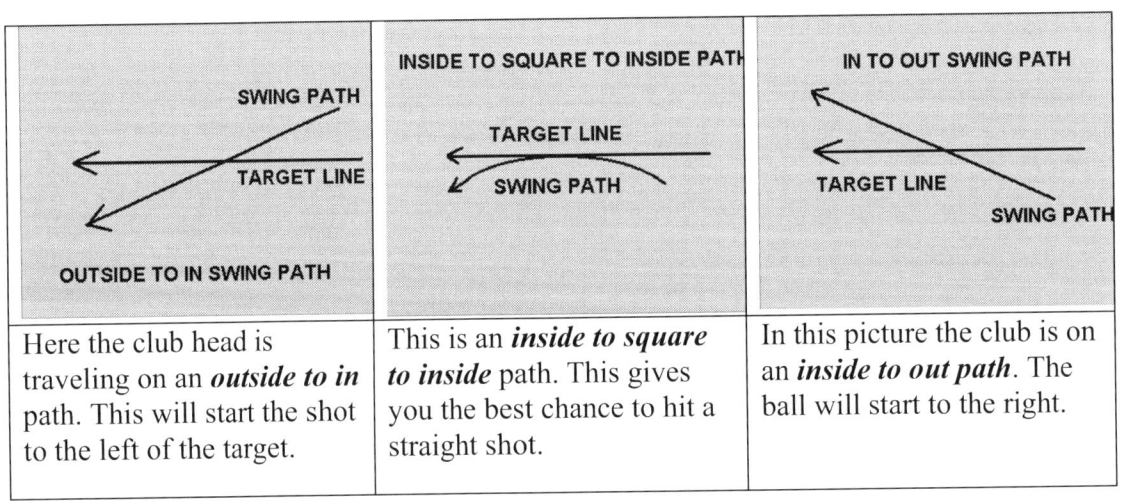

| Here the club head is traveling on an *outside to in* path. This will start the shot to the left of the target. | This is an *inside to square to inside* path. This gives you the best chance to hit a straight shot. | In this picture the club is on an *inside to out path*. The ball will start to the right. |

Try to familiarize yourself with the results produced by various path / face angles as shown in these diagrams. First we'll look at the possibilities when swinging out to in.

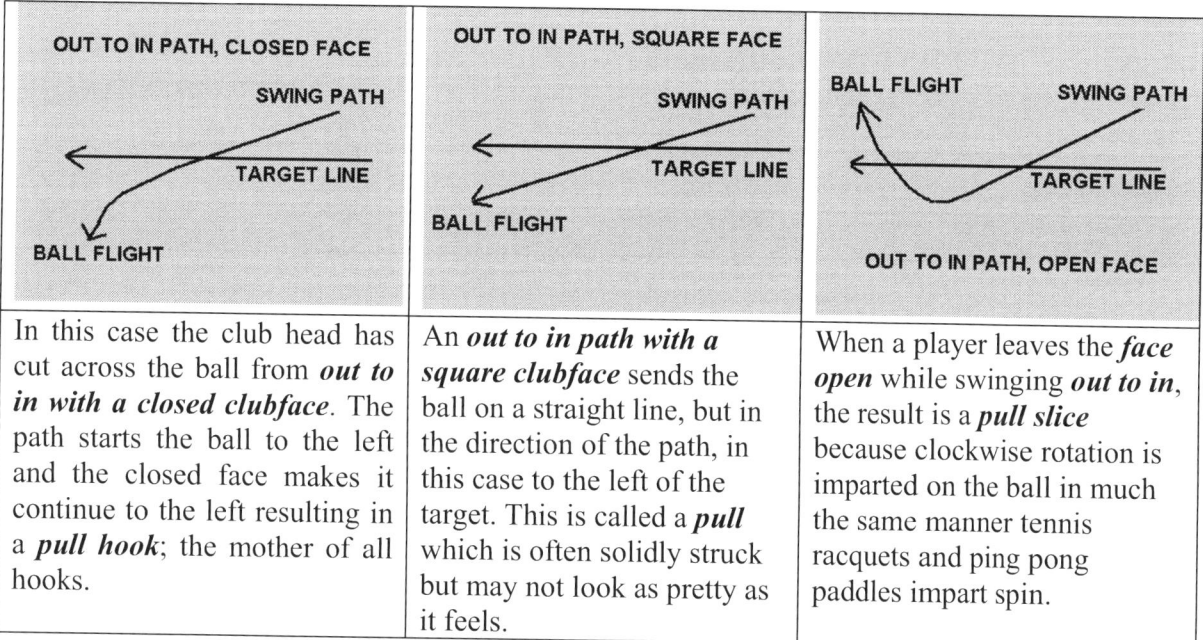

In this case the club head has cut across the ball from **out to in with a closed clubface**. The path starts the ball to the left and the closed face makes it continue to the left resulting in a *pull hook*; the mother of all hooks.	An *out to in path with a square clubface* sends the ball on a straight line, but in the direction of the path, in this case to the left of the target. This is called a *pull* which is often solidly struck but may not look as pretty as it feels.	When a player leaves the *face open* while swinging *out to in*, the result is a *pull slice* because clockwise rotation is imparted on the ball in much the same manner tennis racquets and ping pong paddles impart spin.

Now let's look at what happens when we swing inside to out.

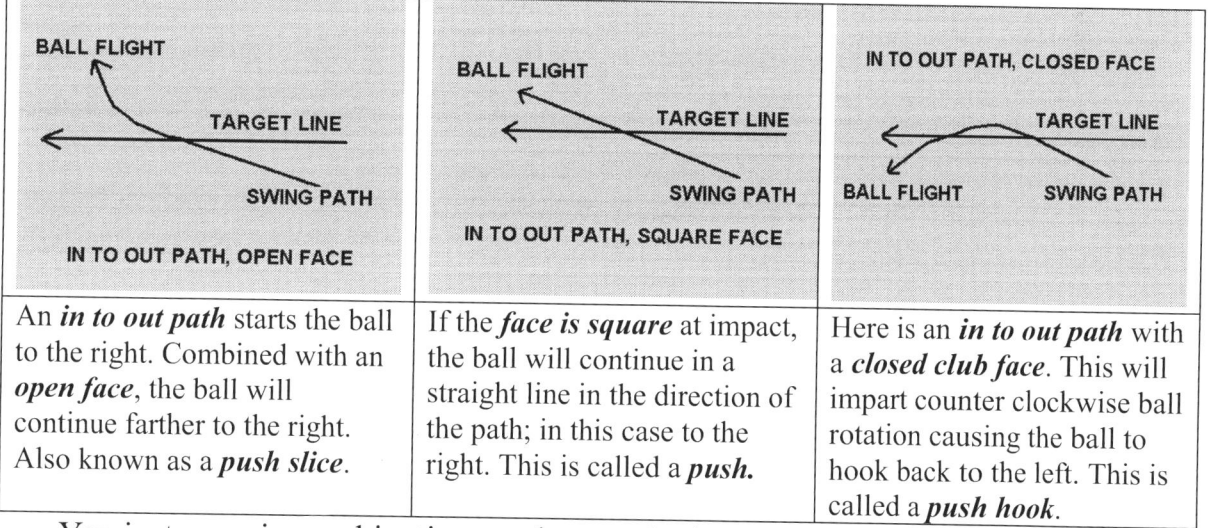

An *in to out path* starts the ball to the right. Combined with an *open face*, the ball will continue farther to the right. Also known as a *push slice*.	If the *face is square* at impact, the ball will continue in a straight line in the direction of the path; in this case to the right. This is called a *push*.	Here is an *in to out path* with a *closed club face*. This will impart counter clockwise ball rotation causing the ball to hook back to the left. This is called a *push hook*.

You just saw six combinations and not a single one produced a straight shot! That's why **we usually try to get people to swing inside square inside but the most important aspect is repeatability**. Do what you can do best and most importantly, consistently.

37

An Inside Approach

There are many devices made to encourage an inside swing path. I believe the one pictured here is one of the most effective. Notice how the club does not approach the ball from straight on. If it did, it would hit the taller pegs on the right. For the club to contact the ball and not hit any pegs, the path will have to be a little from the inside. You might think this path will send the ball to the right, (it could if you overdo it) but the natural rotation of the arms and body will square the clubface to the target.

The **ANGLE OF APPROACH** or attack influences the initial height of a shot. One of the reasons we change ball positions in our stance is to alter the angle of approach.

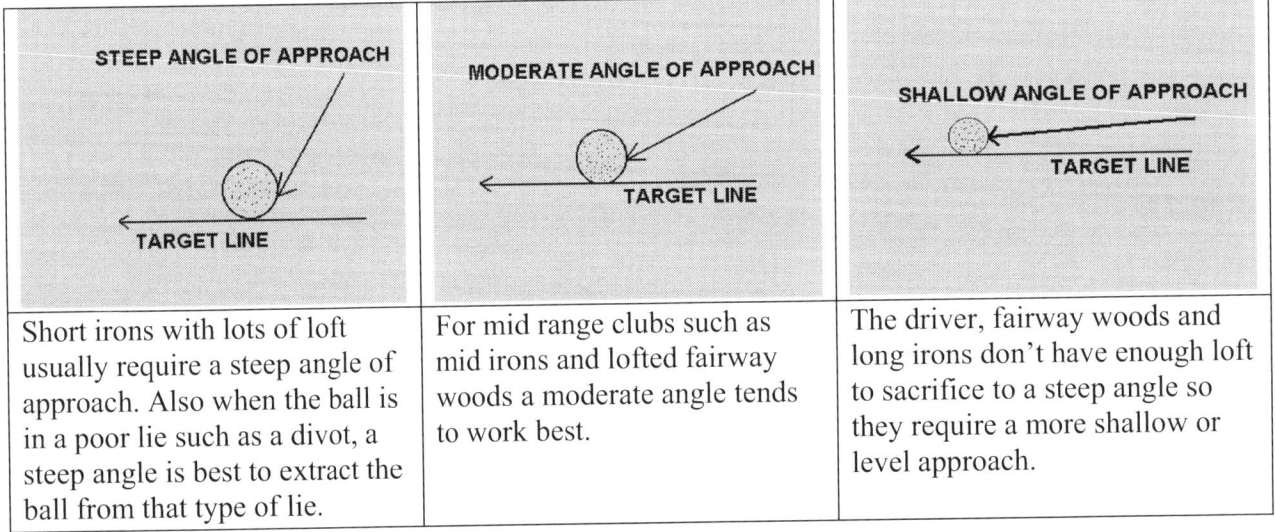

STEEP ANGLE OF APPROACH	MODERATE ANGLE OF APPROACH	SHALLOW ANGLE OF APPROACH
Short irons with lots of loft usually require a steep angle of approach. Also when the ball is in a poor lie such as a divot, a steep angle is best to extract the ball from that type of lie.	For mid range clubs such as mid irons and lofted fairway woods a moderate angle tends to work best.	The driver, fairway woods and long irons don't have enough loft to sacrifice to a steep angle so they require a more shallow or level approach.

The final ball flight law is **CLUB SPEED**. There are many devices that measure club speed in miles per hour. More speed equals more distance. However, there is no substitute for solid, square face contact. Tremendous club speed will actually not help if your shots are being miss hit. It will only make your ball go farther into the woods!

You've just completed physics 101. Congratulations! Before we move into the "how to" part of the full swing, we have to study just a bit of geometry. You need to understand the **SWING PLANE** and how it relates to your technique. Fortunately we have a very scientific device called a hula hoop which helps to illustrate what the plane is.

THE SWING PLANE

The swing plane is described as the tilt of the swing relative to the ground. In baseball and tennis, we swing on a fairly horizontal plane. Games like croquet and cricket require a more vertical plane. The golf swing plane falls somewhere in between, influenced much by the lie angle of the club. The shorter clubs have more upright lie angles requiring you to stand closer to the ball and swing more upright. In contrast, your driver has a much flatter lie angle and due to its length, you must stand farther from the ball and swing more horizontally. *You shouldn't try to consciously change your swing plane from club to club, it should happen naturally, in response to your setup change.*

This is a 6 iron which has a 62 degree lie angle. Notice the hoop is at the same angle.	Halfway into the backswing, the shaft remains parallel to the hoop or, **ON PLANE**. We'd like this same position on the downswing swing too.	Even on the follow through the shaft is on the same plane. See how it lines up with the hoop?

- *Note: In my opinion, a thorough understanding of the swing plane will do wonders for you. Most of my full swing lessons focus on the swing plane, particularly during the downswing and follow through.*

MORE SWING PLANE STUFF

PLEASE BE VERY CAREFUL PRACTICING THIS DRILL.
START WITH THE SHAFTS FARTHER AWAY FROM YOU!!!

| The shafts are on my target line and at the same angle as the lie angle on my club. My takeaway is to the right of, or outside, the shaft. | On the downswing, the club shaft is parallel to the shafts in the ground or, on plane. | The club approaches the ball from under the shaft in the ground. | Notice the club shaft is on plane again during the follow through. |

My favorite way to demonstrate the swing plane is to tee a ball about waist-high and smack it with my driver. In this case I'm swinging on a horizontal plane rather than a tilted one. Notice my body is still "behind" the ball. I wish my real golf swing looked like this at impact!

From this angle, one can clearly see the semi – circular path of the club and how the club approaches the ball from the inside.

I like to envision standing on the straight edge of a protractor or hearth rug and swinging the club along the rounded edge.

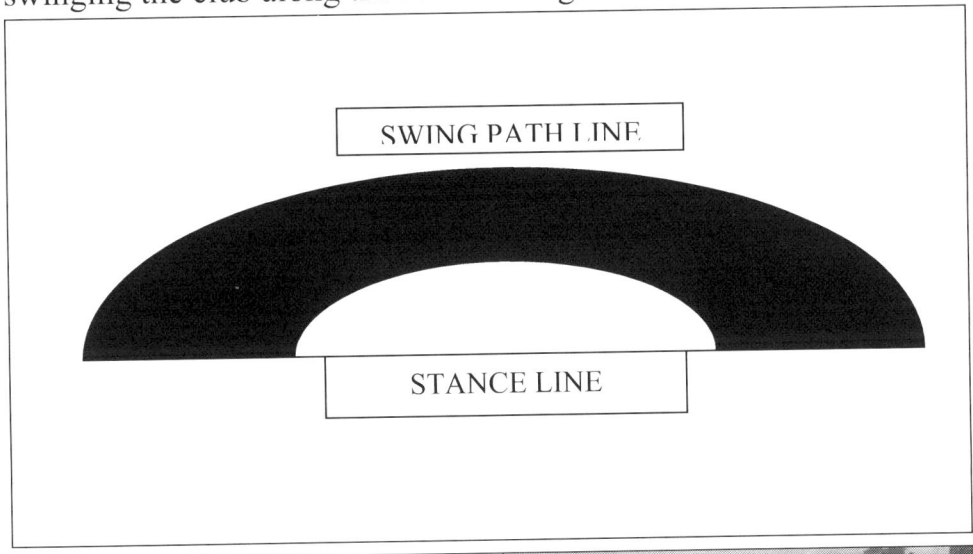

This is the horizontal plane equivalent of swinging outside to in or over the top. Notice my right shoulder is high and has moved out toward the ball. The club head is actually on the other side of the ball. You'd never dream of swinging at a baseball in this manner, would you?

PUTTING INTO ACTION

With our good set up and new found knowledge, let's start swinging the club. Be advised that as you study these photographs, we are simply trying to illustrate various positions that most good players get into. These are basic guidelines and it is strongly suggested you choose one aspect of your swing that needs the most work and focus on it. *Improving one part of the swing will likely improve other parts too*.

THE STARTING POSITION

This is a 6 iron set up. The arms form the **TRIANGLE**, the ball is slightly forward of center and the weight is evenly distributed. Notice the left arm and shaft form a straight line and that my left foot is turned slightly toward the target.	From this angle, notice most of the bending is at the hips. The spine is about perpendicular to the shaft and the arms hang freely. The feet, knees, hips and shoulders all point in the same direction. The weight is on the balls of my feet.

The boards are there to guide my swing. On the take back, I'd like the club over the board to my right and again when I'm halfway down to the ball. At the top of the backswing, the shaft should be parallel to the board out by the ball. As I follow through, the shaft should be over the board to my left. You probably won't lay any boards on the ground but you can imagine a line across the front of your toes and use that as the "roadmap" for your swing.

RELAX, RELAX, RELAX
Not enough can be said for relaxing! Let the air out of your shoulders!

THE TAKEAWAY

During the takeaway, the lower body remains quiet while the chest turns back. The **TRIANGLE** is still intact and the wrists are starting to cock.

The shaft is parallel to the boards in front of my toes and to the board out by the golf ball. Imagine shaking hands with someone standing to your right or "putting the club in the catcher's mitt." Keep the arms in front of the chest.

Here are a few things to watch out for on your takeaway.

1. Starting the club too far inside, behind the body makes it difficult to shift the weight properly.	2. The shaft will "cross the line" or point to the right of the target at the top. The swing will have to be re-routed from here.	1. When the swing starts too much to the outside, the arms "separate" from the body distorting the arms / body relation created at address.	2. The shaft will tend to "lay off" or point to the left of the target at the top. The face will likely be open here and once again the swing will need to be re-routed.

CAUTION! Your lower body should be quiet on the backswing but if you lack flexibility it's okay to move a little. Your hips should turn a bit, just don't let them slide.

THE TOP

At the top of the backswing my lower body has remained stable while the upper body has coiled and shifted onto my right side. The left arm and shaft form the **"L."** Note the gap between my hands and head. That's more powerful than trying to take the club back farther.

From this angle the right elbow is down and not too far behind me. The **TRIANGLE** is now formed by the forearms and the shaft remains parallel to the boards.

One thing to avoid at the top is the dreaded **REVERSE PIVOT**. This is when the body tilts to the left instead of turning to the right. Notice the left shoulder is low, the right hip is high and the right side of the torso is slanted toward the target. This position leads to a number of train wrecks throughout the rest of the swing.

Be sure not to **OVERSWING** as you go back. This is a false feeling of power when really all that's happened is the arms have collapsed and allowed the club to "flop" at the top. From here you'll have to use the first half of the forward swing just to put the club back in position. Try to keep your hands away from your head.

Following are a few ways to help you get the feel for proper weight distribution at the top of the backswing.

1. From a good setup posture, place your left thumb in your sternum with your elbow pointing left.

2. Now turn your upper body onto your right side till your left elbow points in front of you. Don't let your arm move independently. It should move with the chest. This should put you in a good, "loaded" position.

Another good way to feel the proper turn and shift on the backswing is to imagine someone has called out your name from behind your right side and you turn to acknowledge them. Obviously your head won't turn as much when actually swinging.

My favorite is to simply swing back with only the right hand holding the club. Take it back to where you would feel most powerful if you could use only your right arm. In all likelihood, your elbow will fold and you'll maintain a gap between your hand and head at the top. Now reach over and place your left hand on the club. There is no need to swing back any farther.

Here are two more drills to help you learn how to turn your weight properly on the backswing. By now, you must realize the importance of this move since we're spending so much time working on it.

| Position the club in front of your chest. | Rotate to your right keeping the club and arms in the same position. | From here you should be able to drop the club to your waist without hitting your right hip. |

If you do hit your hip, you've swayed your lower body, not turned your upper body

SET UP WITH SQUARE SHOULDERS

| A line across the shoulders should be parallel to the stance and target lines. You want to be cognizant of your left shoulder through your peripheral vision. | Here the shoulders are open or pointed left. The right side will be in the way of the backswing which will likely lead to a reverse pivot. | I hate to say I told you so! Notice the high right hip, low left shoulder and most of the weight on the left side. No chance here! |

THE DOWNSWING

The success of the move back down to the golf ball is largely dependent on your position at the top. Be sure to treat the change of direction or, *transition*, delicately. If you try to change directions quickly, you will likely expend much of your stored power prior to contact.

Here the club has dropped into position to deliver the club head to the ball. Note the "L" formed by the left arm and shaft is still there. The lower body is driving forward while the hips are turning. The head stays behind the ball.

The lower body is starting to turn left while the back is still to the target. **This is more "inside" than I prefer.** The ball will start a little right so I'll need to use my hands a bit to square the face. I guess that's one reason I teach, instead of play, for a living!

For a straight shot, the shaft should be parallel to the boards. ^

Look up **"OVER THE TOP"** in the dictionary and you'll see this: The club has been pushed out toward the golf ball and is getting ready to cut across in a big time outside to in swing path.

Swinging over the top also causes the wrists to un-cock early **(CASTING)** causing a huge power leak. Notice the "L" is gone and the right shoulder is higher than the left.

CONTACT

This is the one part of the swing that we'd like to execute perfectly every time!

Now you can see why we spent so much time working on the **TRIANGLE** in the short game. Note the left arm and shaft form a straight line, the head is behind the ball, the hips are turning left and the right knee is driving toward the target.

Open hips, square shoulders. A good combination to have at impact. The hands are still about the same distance from the body and the shaft is on plane. The right heel is starting to leave the ground. The club has approached from the inside. Some people actually hit the board first because of swinging from the outside.

Yech! Remember the **KILLER MOVE?** If you don't, here's a friendly reminder. After casting the club head on the downswing, it arrives at the ball ahead of the handle. There is virtually no power remaining in this swing.

FOLLOW THROUGH / RELEASE

Because the body has rotated toward the target, the arms are able to stay in front of my chest and retain the **TRIANGLE.** Notice the right hand "shaking hands" with the target.

From this side you can see the body has fully **PIVOTED.** The club is working back over to the board along my stance line; an inside to square to inside path.

Here's a chicken wing Colonel Sanders would be proud to serve! This is what happens when we swing outside to in and neglect to pivot. The left arm has no room so it collapses and destroys the triangle.

From this angle you can see the left elbow poking out. You can also see the lower body has done very little indicating an arms dominant swing. It's tough to be consistent this way.

- To avoid "winging it" through impact, imagine your arms rotating in the same manner they would when steering a car to the left.
- As in the short game, the left wrist stays firm but it will rotate. Imagine *"Hitchhiking in England"* with your left arm.
- Some other thoughts to sense the proper release are to *"Catch Raindrops in Your Left Hand*, *"Hide the Logo on Your Glove"* or *"Turn the Doorknob."*

FINISH

BALANCE is the key ingredient. The front of the body should be vertical, the right knee covers the left knee and the right foot is gently resting on the toes. Nearly all the weight should have turned on to the left side by now.

There's the right foot giving us the "11 Spike Salute." A sign of a controlled and balanced flow of motion. Not a violent hack at the ball.

OUCH! This is an all too familiar pose. Because the arms have dominated the swing, the weight has remained on the right side. That's a lot of power that never made it toward the target, not to mention a strain on the back.

It's not much prettier from this side either. More often than not, this result is simply from trying to hit the ball too hard.

The most important aspects of a good golf swing are having a smooth, balanced motion and proper coordination between the body and arms. When one part of the body tries to outdo the other, the results are usually unfavorable. To teach yourself to use your body and arms together, practice the following drills.

THE SOCCER BALL
The best drills are the simplest ones!

While standing in your address position, hold a soccer size ball on either side of it.

Gently toss the ball to someone to your right. Note how your weight shifts. Have that person throw the ball back to you.

Now turn and throw the ball to the person to your left. Note the synchronization of the body and arms. There's no chicken wing or **KILLER MOVE** here. Do this approximately 30 million times then try swinging a golf club with the same motion.

THE BELLY BUTTON

Place the butt end of the club in your belly button and hold down on the shaft so your arms are extended.	Turn to your right keeping your feet planted.	Now quickly turn to your left, allowing your right foot to come all the way up on its tiptoes. You should feel your arms and hands doing nothing. They move because of the body rotation or **PIVOT**.

THE TASKMASTER

Stand between two tables and place a heavy object on the table to your right. Turn to pick up the object and place it on the table to your left. You'll find it's much easier to move if you use your body. Look how the body made the same **PIVOT** as in the golf swing. Now turn around and do it again. And again. And again. And again……………

Here are some more full swing drills to help you become more consistent.

THE WALL

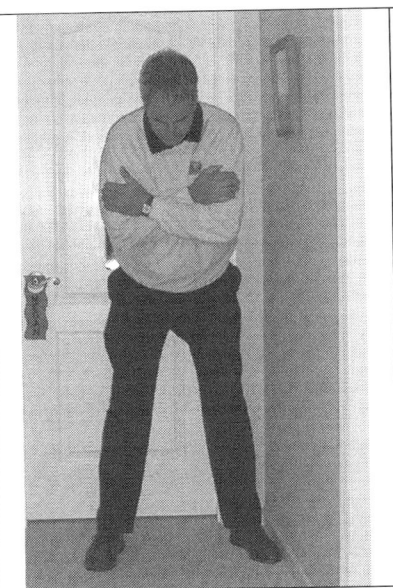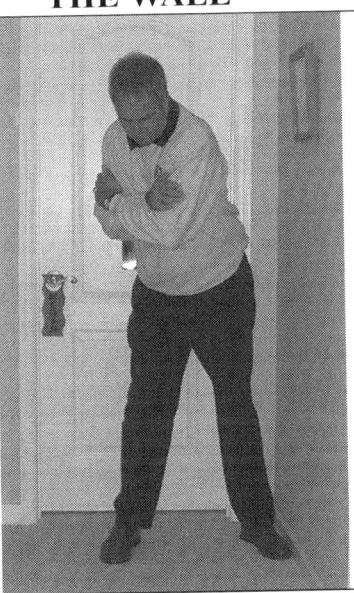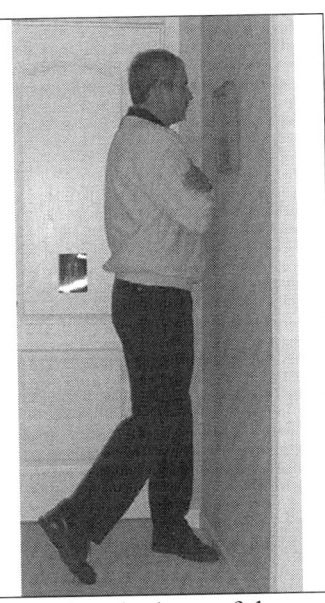

Start from your address position with the outside of your left foot touching the base of the wall. Notice your upper body is farther away from the wall. With your arms crossed in front of your chest, turn back to your right, then quickly turn through and face the wall. The intent is to eliminate "SLIDING" into the shot which is when the hips move too far laterally toward the target on the downswing and we're forced to play "catch up" with the hands.

THE WALL, EPISODE II

You should be able to execute the entire golf swing with a wall about a foot behind your heels. This is a great way to keep the arms in front of the body throughout the swing. Watch out for windows!

- **SWINGING WITH YOUR FEET TOGETHER** is a good way to improve balance and sense the arms swinging freely. Don't use more than a 6 iron. You may want to put the ball on a tee.
- **WHOOSH!** To increase club head speed, hold your driver on the opposite end, where the shaft is skinniest, and swing the grip end of the club through the air. Try to get the club to make a loud, whooshing noise as it travels through the impact area.

WAIST HIGH, TOE UP TO WAIST HIGH, TOE UP

Place 2 woods on the ground on your stance line. The wood to your right should be facing in front of you, the wood to your left should face behind you.

On your takeaway, your club should be directly over the club on the ground and the clubface in the same position. The shaft is waist high and the toe of the club points up.

The same goes for the follow through. And again, The shaft is waist high and the toe of the club points up.

PVC OVERKILL

This is what can happen if you sniff too much PVC cement! Actually this is an all purpose swing trainer I made myself. The tube between my feet slides back and forth so I can comfirm ball position. The tubes in the foreground guide my swing plane. The long tube in front of my feet directs my takeaway and follow through. To my sides are attachments to keep from swaying my hips going back and sliding them coming through. The tube behind my head keeps me from taking the club too far back to the inside.

| In this position, I want the shaft parallel to the longest tube on the ground. | As I start down, the club stays to my side with the shaft parallel to the slanted tubes or "on plane." | Now the club can swing under the slanted tubes or, from the inside. | My **PIVOT** has maneuvered the club back over my stance line. |

THE OVER AND UNDER

Sounds like a bet you'd place in Vegas. There are many ways to get rid of an over the top downswing. This is an effective, albeit difficult, drill.

The club swings back to the outside of the tube….

…and under the tube as it approaches the ball.

ANOTHER PIVOT DRILL

Start with the shaft firmly pressed against both legs, above the knee.

Turn to your left, keeping the shaft on both legs. Your lower body will bring your upper body around.

Guard against the shaft coming off your right leg. This indicates too much upper body motion.

III. TROUBLE SHOTS

If you've read this far, you shouldn't have any need for this chapter! However, you may have a friend who does, so you'd better read on.

This chapter will deal with various situations in the sand, trees, rough, etc. I prefer to call them *"recovery shots"* which at least makes it sound like we have a chance!

GREENSIDE BUNKERS

Bunker shots needn't be all that difficult. It's a lot like a pitch shot, only a little faster swing. Besides, how often do you get to miss the ball on purpose? **The most important requirement is getting the club to bottom out in the right spot**. If you can do that, the ball will simply "surf" on the wave of sand you create with the swing.

Make sure you have a decent sand wedge, it helps. If you play from deep, fluffy sand, you'll probably want a wedge with a lot of bounce. Harder, firmer sand requires less bounce. Simply stated, the bounce is how much lower the trailing edge of the bottom of the club is compared to the leading edge.

Remember, this is actually a short game shot so the setup will be much like pitching. Weight left, stance a little open.

The first thing to do is to develop a consistent bottom to the swing. Draw a line in the sand and straddle the line so it is in the middle of your stance. Keeping your weight anchored on the left side, make some full swings and see if you can get the club to bottom out right at the line. You want to imagine the ball is just to the left of the line. Keep practicing till you have a nice, long, shallow sand divot that begins at the line. The sand should be flying high and far.

- You're not allowed to "ground" your club in the sand because bunkers are considered hazards. Make sure the club hovers above the sand while addressing the ball.

| Play the ball a little left of center with your weight on your left side and your hands about even with the ball. | Aim just a little left of the target and bring the club up at a steep angle, cocking the wrists early in the backswing. | The "L" is created early in the backswing to encourage swinging downward into the sand. |

| Aim to make contact behind (to the right of) the ball. We don't want to contact the ball at all. Just let the sand take it out. | Much like the full swing, the body should **PIVOT** and the arms should extend. Don't be suckered into stopping at the ball! | Go ahead and take it right through to a "camera ready" finish. The more you can treat this like a regular shot, the easier it becomes. |

You may have noticed there has been no mention of an extremely open clubface at address, digging the feet in, aiming way left and swinging out to in on purpose. There are techniques which require these actions but they are too complicated. ***Your primary concern is to get out of the bunker and onto the green!*** I will often demonstrate using a putter and a buried lie. As long as you can displace the sand surrounding the ball, it shouldn't matter what club you use!

- For a buried lie, close the clubface a little. It will dig in more easily.
- For hard or wet sand, swing easier and consider using a pitching wedge so it will dig and not bounce.

THE ALMIGHTY DOLLAR

Envision the golf ball sitting on top of George Washington's portrait on a dollar bill. Then aim to remove a stack of bills. Don't hit George!

THE SHELL GAME

TEE IT UP

This is a trick we sometimes play on our students. We ask them to take a swing at each pile of sand and try to make the sand land on the green. What they don't know is that there is a ball in the third pile. It almost always flies out high and softly.

Here we've sunk a tee in the sand under the golf ball. Practice knocking the tee out from under the ball and your club will bottom out in the right place more often.

THE RAKE

Here the rake has been positioned with the teeth to the right of the ball.	That's to encourage me to keep the "L" between my left arm and club shaft on the downswing.	If we envision "scooping" the ball out of the bunker, we lose the "L" and bottom out too early, knocking a few teeth out!

FAIRWAY BUNKERS

This is another shot that doesn't have to be difficult. As in most cases, it's simply a matter of knowing what to do and getting over the "fear factor." Here's how to get out of a fairway bunker.

- Look at the lie. If it's in a footprint, be realistic. Just get it back on the fairway! Now look at the required trajectory to get it out of the bunker. Don't be greedy! Take plenty of loft to get it over the lip.
- This shot is much like using an iron when the ball is on the turf. ***You should contact the ball first, on the downswing, then the sand.*** You might even take as much sand as you did in the greenside bunker, *after* you contact the ball.
- Work your feet into the sand just a little. This will stabilize your base.
- Play the ball about in the center of your stance.
- Keep the lower body as quiet as possible on the backswing. This is to keep from over swinging and to maintain posture.
- Your PIVOT will be somewhat restricted because it's easy to slip in the sand.
- Swing easier than normal. Balance and solid contact are vital.
- PRACTICE! This is probably the least practiced of all shots.
- A high lofted fairway wood or hybrid works nicely here.

ROUGH

This is when strength in the hands, wrists and forearms can be helpful. The long grass grabs the club, slowing it down and twisting it closed. To test your strength, hold an ordinary bathroom scale and see how many pounds of pressure you can squeeze. Ladies should shoot for 100 pounds. Men should try for 150.

When escaping the rough, do the following: 1. Open the clubface a little, the long grass tends to twist it closed 2. Hold the club tighter. 3. Play the ball slightly back in the stance. 4. Hover the club above the ground while addressing the ball.
5. Swing the club up at a steep angle on the back swing.
Swing down at a steep descent trying to get the club in and out of the rough as quickly as possible. If you try to sweep the ball from long grass, the club will get stuck. Don't be heroic. Use plenty of loft and expect a shorter, lower shot than normal.

UNEVEN LIES

Balance and posture are the keys here. Because you're standing on uneven ground, it's harder to keep your balance. You'll also have to alter your posture somewhat so it is even more important to stay in your address posture throughout the swing. In general, swing easier and focus on good contact and balance when swinging from an uneven lie.

Uphill
- Position ball forward in stance.
- Align shoulders parallel to terrain.
- Use less loft, ball will fly higher.
- Guard against pulling ball to left as pivot will be restricted.

Downhill
- Position ball back in stance.
- Align shoulders parallel to terrain.
- Steep back swing and downswing.
- Let club follow terrain on follow thru.
- Take more loft; ball will fly lower.
- Guard against ball moving to right.

Side hill, ball above feet.
- Stand taller.
- Stand farther from ball.
- Grip down on club.
- Swing "around" body.
- Aim right. Ball will tend to go left.

Side hill, ball below feet.
- More knee flex.
- Stand closer to ball.
- Hold end of club.
- Swing upright
- Aim left. Ball will tend to go right.

TREES

Take it from someone who has been there many times. In most cases it is best to take the safest route back to the fairway from the trees. Cut your losses. Only in the direst of situations should you try to pull off a shot when the odds are against you.

You'll need a low shot to keep the ball under the branches. With a mid iron, play the ball back in your stance with your hands and weight well forward. This will encourage a descending blow and de – loft the club to keep the ball flight low. Grip down on the handle; keep your weight anchored on your left side. Take the club back by cocking your wrists then try to contact the ball with a sharp, descending action. Abbreviate the follow through and keep the wrists firm. (Maintain the **TRIANGLE**.) Watch out! Sometimes we hit this shot so solidly it goes across the fairway to the trees on the other side!

HOOKS AND SLICES

The simplest way to *intentionally* curve the ball is to alter the clubface angle *before* you address the ball. In fact, you should do so before you even grip the club. For a hook, line up in the direction you want the ball to start, then close the clubface until it's pointed where you want the ball to end up. Make your normal swing and the ball will hook. For a slice, align left of the target and open the clubface until it is aimed at the target. Again, make your normal swing. The ball will curve to the right.

| To hook the ball, align to the right and close the clubface. Take less club than you would normally need for the same distance because closing the clubface de-lofts the club. | To slice the ball, align to the left and open the clubface. Take more club than you would normally need from the same distance because opening the clubface adds loft to it. |

WIND

"When it's breezy, swing easy," an old saying that makes a lot of sense. An easier swing will impart less spin on the ball, making it less vulnerable to the wind.

- Widen the stance to keep from being blown over; even when putting.
- To keep the ball lower, play the ball back in your stance.
- Use a ¾ backswing and abbreviated follow through.
- Wind is a difficult element with which to deal. Be patient. Play some par 4's as par 5's and try to take advantage of the downwind holes.
- If you're in a tournament, realize the entire field will likely be posting a higher score than usual.

EXTREME COLD, HEAVY RAIN, SLEET, SNOW

- GET A LIFE!

IV. COURSE MANAGEMENT

Course management is a fancy way of saying "smart golf." It covers everything from club / shot selection to emotional control. At the highest level, smart golf is often what separates the winner from the rest of the field.

- Beginning golfers shouldn't concern themselves with scoring. Focus on making good contact and keeping the ball out of serious trouble.

- If you do keep score, set a personal par. Perhaps double bogey would be an achievable score. On a regulation course, your total par would be 108. If you make a bogey, consider it a birdie.

As your skills improve, you'll be able to manage your game more efficiently because you'll be a better ball striker and can predict your shots more easily. Following are some basic guidelines to help you manage your game.

- Warm up before you play. Enough to get loose.

- Learn, and memorize, how far you can carry the ball with each club.

- Pay close attention to hole locations and yardage markers. A cup on the back of the green could add 20 yards to the shot.

- Do not carry any clubs in your bag in which you have no confidence. You'll only tempt yourself. If this means carrying fewer than 14 clubs, so be it.

- Very rarely should you swing with 100% power. The tour players claim that about ¾ of the shots they hit are partial shots.

- Your driver is which ever club you hit the longest and straightest. Many players with slow swing speed carry the ball farthest with a 3 or 5 wood.

- After executing a shot poorly, it is best to not attempt to follow it with a miraculous one. Cut your losses and get on with your game.

- Don't let other players influence how you play. If you're paired with long hitters, let them blow it by you. A positive approach would be to realize you'll have the first shot at the green, and a chance to put the pressure back on them.

- Try not to get caught up in technique while playing. Save that for the driving range. Take one or two positive swing thoughts to the course.

- If your natural ball flight is left to right, don't fight it. For tee shots, set up on the right side of the tee box, so you'll have plenty of room to aim left and allow for the fade. Avoid attacking flags on the left side of the green. Do the opposite if you play a right to left shot.

- Do your best to forget about poor shots. They're history. This is easier said than done.

- Try not to keep a running score total in your mind. It's tempting to think ahead, but doing so usually leads to disaster.

- In most instances play doglegs wide. Playing too close to the corner can block out your next shot.

- Establish a pre-shot routine:

| Start from behind the ball and envision the shot. Choose the line on which you want the ball to travel. | Align the clubface to the target. Use an intermediate target no more than 3 feet in front of the ball. | Align your body parallel to the target line. Try not to spend an eternity over the ball. If you must, stay in motion to avoid tension. |

- Establish a "personal" par for yourself. Par on the scorecard is for a scratch player.

- When laying up short of trouble, be sure to take a club that has no chance of reaching the trouble.

- Also when laying up, be sure to consider the distance you'll have remaining for your next shot. Try to lay up to your most comfortable distance.

- Check the scorecard or consult the starter for local rules. Sometimes there are drop areas that can save many yards.

- Be careful not to "SHORT SIDE" yourself.

The short side is the side of the green on which the hole is located. In this case, the hole is on the left side, just in front of my head, and I'm aimed a little right of it. A straight shot gives me a chance to make the putt. A slight pull to the left might actually put me closer to the hole. Anything to the right, the "bail out" area, either leaves me a longish putt or an easy 8 iron chip across the green. The area to avoid is left, the short side. Over there the bunker comes into play and a chip or pitch will be difficult because there won't be much room to roll the ball after it lands.

- When you're having "one of those days," slow everything down. Usually our timing is off so take more club than usual and swing easier. This will help you find a rhythm to your swing.

WATCH WHERE THE TEE BOXES ARE AIMED

This teeing ground is aligned toward the right side, where the trouble is. It's easy to be lulled into aligning your shot the same way.	If you follow your pre shot routine, you'll be able to notice where the tee is aligned. Note here the club aims in the middle of the fairway while the body is parallel left.

V. ETIQUETTE

It's not just a matter of being polite and quiet. It's all about how you handle yourself on the course. Common sense is the best approach. Following are a few tips on how to behave on the golf course and to speed up play.

- Arrive on time to play. Don't be tugging on your shoes while hopping up to the first tee.
- Be prepared. Have plenty of tees, golf balls and carry a ball marker and a pitch mark repair tool for the greens.
- Keep an extra golf ball in your pocket. If you lose a ball in the woods or water, you won't have to go back to the cart to get another ball.
- In a friendly game, the "honor" of teeing first is often determined by a toss of a tee. Whomever the tee points to goes first. From then on, the lowest score on the previous hole takes the honor. If the previous hole was tied, go back to the last hole that was won or lost.
- Stand still and keep quiet while others are hitting.
- On the tee, the safest place to stand is in front of and to the player's right.

| These people are standing in the safest place. Nothing's impossible, but if they get hit while standing there, then this lady is a trick shot artist! | Here's an accident (or a fight) waiting to happen! The people far right and left could be hit and the person in the background is in the player's peripheral vision. |

- For shots on the fairway, be careful not to get too far ahead of other players. Be aware of what's going on around you. Don't get caught in the line of fire!
- Replace divots or fill with the mixture provided by the course.

- The order of play is the player farthest from the hole goes first.
- To speed things up, play "ready golf;" which is to proceed with play even if you're not farthest from the hole. Make sure it is safe to do so and won't interfere with other players.

Once you get to the green, a whole new set of rules apply!

- Repair your ball mark and at least one other one.
- Do not step on another player's line.
- Avoid dragging your feet.
- When another player is putting, stand still and out of their vision.
- Avoid casting your shadow across another player's line.
- Use the continuous putting option whenever possible. This means to keep putting till you finish as long as it won't interfere with other players.
- Be ready when it's your turn. Read your putt while someone else is putting.
- Be sure to leave your golf bag or cart between the green and the next tee. This will allow your group to exit the green quickly.
- If you're in charge of keeping scores, wait till the next tee to record them.

Now for some general etiquette:

- Do not offer advice unless someone asks you for it.
- Keep up with the group in front of you. If you can't, let the group behind you play through.
- Be humble. Don't brag about great shots or scores. Play it cool!
- Avoid whining about misfortune. We all get bad breaks.

And finally:

- If you find yourself often playing golf with someone you just don't enjoy, find another playing partner!

VI. EXERCISES

This chapter really should appear in the front of the book. If I knew how to change it in the computer, I would! It is no secret that physical fitness has become a huge part of championship golf. Added strength and flexibility can do wonders for your game. Most health clubs now have golf specific training programs. Anything you can do to improve your physical fitness is wonderful. Following are a few of the stretching exercises we do in our golf schools. Be careful not to aggravate any existing injuries.

Stretch an arm out in front of you and pull back on your fingers.	Next, pull the fingers downward.	Now try pulling the fingers down with your palm up.	Now grab the arm at the elbow and pull it toward you. Repeat all four with the other arm.

Thumbs on your temples. Fingertips on top of your head. By that way, that's a tree behind me, not a wig that I'm wearing!	Now squish your elbows together and hold it for a few seconds. (You may want to do this one where no one can see you!)	Place a few fingers on the side of your chin.	Turn your head to stretch the neck muscles. Repeat in other direction.

A weighted club makes a great training aid. Simply swinging it back and forth will groove a good, smooth swing and strengthen the proper muscles. You can purchase weighted clubs or weights that fit on the end of a club. If you have an old club with a steel shaft, you can cut off the grip and fill the shaft with sand or lead shot. Be sure to stuff something down the shaft to hold the sand in place, and then install a new grip. You can even spiral lead tape up and down the shaft. The club should weigh about 30 ounces, heavier if you can handle it.

Club behind you, in your fingertips, palms facing out.	Lean forward and raise your arms. Hold it for a few seconds.	Club behind body, over left shoulder. Right hand on top.	Repeat on other side.

Shaft across back of neck. Rotate to your right keeping the lower body still and eyes focused on golf ball. Make sure shaft stays level.	Turn in other direction. Try to get as much trunk rotation in both directions while the lower body resists.	Without tilting excessively, reach way down with one hand and way up with the other. Repeat on the other side.

 Here's one with a bit of a twist. Hold your club in front of you.	 Right arm over left arm.	 Left arm over right arm.

 With a club in your hands, stretch your arms out in front you.	 Now reach over your head and back as far as you can.

VII. PRACTICE

Attaining your highest possible achievement level in golf requires a tremendous commitment of time, effort, desire and patience. To truly see gradual improvement, one must practice at least 3 times a week and preferably more. Depending on your current level, expect to attain your goals in no less than three years. Bear in mind that during that time, there will be many peaks and valleys. Sometimes you'll play worse than when you started and other times the game will seem easy. One must accept that this is the nature of golf and one of the many things that makes it so interesting.

HOW TO PRACTICE

Everyone has different ways of practicing. Some enjoy being totally isolated in their own little world not only to help them concentrate, but for the solitude itself. Others like to be in the midst of it all and enjoy having some commotion around them. Probably a mix of these environments is best. We all need a quiet area particularly when working on new things, but the game itself is played in front of others so we need to learn to perform at our best even if there is potential for distraction. Many enjoy practicing with one other person, especially someone who knows their swing. Not only can that person be an extra pair of eyes for you, he can also be a friendly competitor for putting contests, closest to the flag, etc.

STRETCHING

Always stretch for at least five minutes before starting a practice session. You don't have to partake in a major workout, just do some simple exercises to limber up and help prevent injury.

PUTTING

Work mostly on your routine and distance control. I often practice using just one ball to simulate a real game. Challenge yourself. Devise drills such as making ten four footers in a row, or a certain percentage of longer putts. Do anything that will toughen you mentally and prepare you for the pressure of a real match.

CHIPPING

The largest factor for club selection is not how far from the green your ball sits but how much green you have for the ball to roll on. In general, use more loft for less green and less loft for more green. Find a fairly flat chip shot of about 40 feet and set up no more than 3 club lengths from the edge of the green. Usually an 8 iron works well for this shot but try it with a 4 iron all the way up to a sand wedge. Take note of how far the ball rolls after it lands. This is called the roll to carry ratio (RTCR) and will help you for shot and club selection on the course. Remember if you're chipping from long grass you may need to swing faster so more loft will likely be needed.

Once you've established your RTCR's, practice different scenarios such as uphill, downhill, side hill, tight grass, long grass, etc. Even include shots where the ball is resting on the collar but is up against the longer grass of the fringe. You may consider a fairway wood or flange of a sand wedge for this shot.

As with any chip shot, your goal is to sink it and settle for being close. Keep track of the percentage of chip shots that stop inside 3 feet from the hole.

PITCHING AND SAND

Good wedge play is arguably the single most important part of golf. Being able to pitch the ball close to the hole makes putting much easier and takes pressure of your long game. Practice in a similar manner to chipping, creating as many different shots as possible.

It is good to combine your chipping, pitching and sand practice with putting. Using no more than 3 balls from any certain spot, chip or pitch the balls as close as you can, then putt each ball into the hole. Keep track of your "up & down" percentages. Do at least 20 repetitions.

FULL WEDGES

It is estimated that 75% of golf is played from inside 100 yards, much of that from just outside pitching range but inside short iron range, hence the need for full wedge shots. Practice these shots in groups of 3 balls in 5 yard increments starting at 50 yards up to 100 yards then work back down to 50. Do at least twice.

Use different lofts if desired and alter the distances to your ability.

IRONS
Start with the short irons and work your way to the long irons, then back to the short. You may consider using odd numbered clubs one day and even numbered the next. In addition to standard shots be sure to save some time for practicing knock downs, punches, fades, draws etc. It is also good to practice hitting a little harder and softer than usual for times when you are in between clubs on the golf course.

WOODS and TEE SHOTS
In addition to hitting fairway woods off the ground, practice tee shots with them for long par threes and tight driving holes. Create an imaginary fairway on the range and hit 14 drives to it. Count how many stay in. You should be able to get at least 10!

TROUBLE SHOTS
Focus primarily on good balance and solid contact from uneven lies and fairway bunkers. Take a little more club and swing easier. Practice 10 shots from the fairway bunker, uphill, downhill and side hill lies.

GENERAL TIPS

- Practice at a slow pace. Most people just rapid fire range balls and don't accomplish anything other than a little exercise.

- The best time to practice is after playing so what you need to work on is fresh in your mind.

- Always use your pre shot routine when practicing so these habits carry over to the course.

- Set up a practice station with one club between your feet and the ball parallel to the target line for alignment and another club perpendicular to the target line for ball position.

- Determine how far you can comfortably carry the ball with each club.

- Don't practice only from perfect lies.

- Research indicates that quantity can be good too. The more you practice, the better you'll become.

PLAYING

- Play with others who are better players than you are.

- Putt everything in. No gimmes!

- Play the ball as it lies.

- Do not attempt to hit a shot you've never practiced.

- Play a round of golf on the range. Pretend you are playing a course and recreate each hole. Start with the opening tee shot, then hit the shot you would likely need for the second shot and so on. This will make practicing more like playing.

The next page is the form we use at Steve Dresser Golf Academy when we give playing lessons. In addition to scorecard information we track fairways hit, number of putts, and greens in regulation. We like to track the number of shots to and from the 100 yard marker. For better players, we use the 150 marker and the 50 marker for beginners. You may photo copy this for your own use or make modifications. Once you've compiled 10 scores, do an analysis of total greens, putts, etc. to pinpoint your strengths and weaknesses.

PLAYING LESSON EVALUATION

NAME_____HANDICAP_____DATE_____COURSE_____

RATING_____SLOPE_____CONDITIONS_____

HOLE	PAR	YDGE	SCORE	FWY?	# SHOTS TO 100	# SHOTS FROM 100	PUTTS	GIR?	UP&DOWN?	COMMENTS
1										
2										
3										
4										
5										
6										
7										
8										
9										
OUT										
10										
11										
12										
13										
14										
15										
16										
17										
18										
IN										
TOTAL										

PLAYING TENDENCIES

ALIGNMENT:_____
CLUB/SHOT
SELECTION_____

ROUTINE_____

RECOMMENDATIONS_____
_____

VIII. EQUIPMENT

Your golf equipment can make a world of difference in your game. You needn't spend a fortune to be properly fit. In our golf schools, we use an exclusive software program that calculates exact specifications for all types of players. Following are the characteristics of club design and assembly that we take into consideration.

- **LENGTH**
- **SHAFT MATERIAL**
- **SHAFT WEIGHT**
- **SHAFT FLEX**
- **SHAFT FREQUENCY**
- **SHAFT KICK POINT**
- **LIE ANGLE**
- **LOFT ANGLE**
- **FACE ANGLE**
- **CLUB HEAD DESIGN**
- **CENTER OF GRAVITY**
- **GRIP SIZE**
- **GRIP MATERIAL**
- **TOTAL WEIGHT**
- **SWING WEIGHT**

To fit the above specifications properly, we need a profile of the customer. Following are some of the ingredients that make up the profile.

- **HEIGHT**
- **BUILD**
- **STRENGTH**
- **EXPERIENCE**
- **SWING STYLE**
- **CLUB SPEED**
- **BALL SPEED**
- **CARRY DISTANCE**
- **TEMPO**

The other major factor is set make up. Years ago our choices were limited but now it's not uncommon to see a set with more woods or hybrids than irons or with extra wedges. This is an important aspect of club fitting that should be considered carefully.

IX. RULES

The rules of golf are extensive and confusing but they really are designed to help you. There are a few basic rules everyone should know without consulting the rule book. In tournament golf, if you're unsure what to do, ask for a rules official.

OUT OF BOUNDS
O. B., re-tee, hit 3! This one's plain and simple. If your ball goes out of bounds, you must replay the shot from the same spot counting the shot that went O. B. and adding a penalty stroke. Out of bounds is usually identified with white stakes. If you're not sure whether or not you're O.B. you may hit a provisional ball. If you find the original ball is in bounds, you may continue playing it without penalty.

UNPLAYABLE LIE
You may declare any shot unplayable and exercise one of three options. 1. You may drop the ball within two club lengths of where it lays no closer to the hole. 2. You may use the line of sight rule which means you picture a line from the hole back to your ball and drop farther back on that line as far as you want, as long as you stay in bounds. 3. You may replay the shot. All options come with a penalty stroke.

- *A handy rules tip to remember when taking a drop is if there is no penalty involved you are allowed one club length relief. If there is a penalty, two club lengths are permitted.*

- Free drop from cart paths, ground under repair, casual water, and manmade obstructions. Find the nearest point of relief, drop within one club length. Sometimes the nearest point of relief is worse than the existing situation. I've hit many a shot right from the cart path.

WATER HAZARD

When the hazard is directly in the line of play, it will be marked with yellow stakes. You have three options. 1. Take off the shoes and socks, roll up the pants legs and play it! No penalty. Remember not to ground the club. That's two strokes! 2. Most often, you will exercise the line of sight rule. Keep the point where the ball last crossed the hazard between you and the hole and go back as far as you'd like. One penalty stroke. 3. Replay the shot. One penalty stroke.

LATERAL WATER HAZARD

When the hazard sits to the side of the line of play, it is called a lateral hazard and will be marked with red stakes and or paint. You get the same three options as the regular hazard plus two more. The oft used option is to drop the ball within two club lengths of where it entered the hazard, no closer to the hole. You may also drop the ball on the other side of the hazard at a point equidistant from the hole. Both options require a penalty stroke.

LOST BALL, OUTSIDE A HAZARD

Occasionally golf balls are lost in areas other than water hazards such as deep woods or long grass. Because there are no yellow or red stakes, there is no way to determine where to drop the ball. The only choice is to replay the shot, counting the first one and adding a penalty stroke. It's practically the same as hitting out of bounds. You're permitted to hit a provisional ball. Be sure you declare it is a provisional or you'll have to play that ball even if you find the first one. Also be sure the ball is indeed not in a hazard or you'll have to play the provisional ball.

X. ACKNOWLEDGMENTS

Over the years I've learned golf through trial and error, books, videos, seminars, observation and lessons. Along the way I've had some excellent advice from many wonderful people. I'd like to mention a few of them and thank them for helping me with my game and career.

- First I need to thank my dad, Pete Dresser, "Clubmaker to the Stars" for introducing me to the game and for having the wisdom to have someone else teach me!

- That someone else was Joe Kirkwood, a world renowned trick shot artist and 13 time winner on the PGA tour. Thanks Joe, for sharing your *passion* for the game.

- Thanks to Peggy Kirk Bell, a Golf Digest Top 100 Teacher, for giving me *confidence* in my ability.

- Larry Startzel was our club pro when I was a teenager. In addition to helping me improve, I thank Larry for teaching me to *respect* the game.

- Jim Beckett and I worked together at a golf school in the 1980's. At first, I thought our philosophies were miles apart. After a while, I realized he made a lot of sense. I thank Jim for *"demystifying"* (as he would say) the golf swing.

- Thanks to Billy Delk with whom I worked for 11 years at Steve Dresser Golf Academy. He helped me establish our program and taught me a lot of the *finer points* of the swing.

- Thanks also to Eileen Kask, a PGA Professional who joined our staff in 2004 and has been a wonderful addition to the team!

Steve Dresser is originally from Stowe, Vermont and has been teaching golf for over 25 years. He is a Class A member of the PGA and recipient of the prestigious Palmer Maples Teacher of the Year award from the Carolinas Section of the PGA for 2004. He is also a Golf Magazine Top Regional Teacher and is annually recognized by Golf Digest as one of the top instructors in South Carolina. He and his wife Terry have operated Steve Dresser Golf Academy in Pawleys Island, South Carolina since 1989.

For information about Steve Dresser Golf Academy go to www.dressergolf.com or call 1 800 397 2678.

Made in the USA
Charleston, SC
22 April 2014